Get comfortable in the kitchen with more than 100 impossible-to-mess-up recipes.

Cooking can often be time-consuming, expensive, wasteful, and stressful for those who are not practiced in the kitchen. In *Meals You Can't Mess Up*, food and travel writer Shay Spence sets out to eliminate the four greatest recipe pain points—long prep and cook times, too many expensive ingredients, lots of chopping, and a mess of dishes at the end—with recipes that are as foolproof as possible.

No recipe in this cookbook calls for more than ten ingredients, most can be cooked in just one pot or pan (never more than two), and few take more than thirty minutes from start to finish. But prioritizing ease doesn't mean ignoring flavor. With dishes like Burst Tomato-Basil Tortellini with Burrata and Beer Cheese Broccoli Orzo Soup, Shay's ingenious dishes bring unexpected twists to classic combinations.

You'll find calm in the kitchen as you whip up one easy dish after the other, and if you don't . . . well, at least now you know some super-quick, easy recipes to get you out of there as soon as possible.

meals you can't mess up

meals you can't mess up

SHAY SPENCE

DK

DK | Penguin Random House

Publisher Mike Sanders
Executive Editor Alexander Rigby
Art & Design Director William Thomas
Editorial Director Ann Barton
Assistant Director of Art & Design Becky Batchelor
Editorial Assistant Resham Anand
Recipe Photographer Mackenzie Smith
Lifestyle Photographer Romi Burianova
Food Stylist Maite Aizpurua
Prop Stylist Maura Cusick
Recipe Tester Bee Berrie & Janet McCracken
Developmental Editor Jennifer Hope Choi
Copyeditor Tiffany Taing
Proofreaders Bianca Bosman & Mira S. Park
Indexer Johnna VanHoose Dinse

First American Edition, 2026
Published in the United States by DK Publishing
1745 Broadway, 20th Floor, New York, NY 10019

The authorized representative in the EEA is Dorling Kindersley Verlag GmbH. Arnulfstr. 124, 80636 Munich, Germany

26 27 28 29 10 9 8 7 6 5 4 3 2 1
001-349389-SEP2026

A catalog record for this book is available from the Library of Congress.
ISBN 978-0-5939-6871-0

DK books are available at special discounts when purchased in bulk for sales promotions, premiums, fund-raising, or educational use. For details, contact SpecialSales@dk.com

Printed and bound in China

www.dk.com

FSC www.fsc.org MIX Paper | Supporting responsible forestry FSC™ C018179

This book was made with Forest Stewardship Council™ certified paper – one small step in DK's commitment to a sustainable future.
Learn more at **www.dk.com/uk/information/sustainability**

To my incredible parents,
who didn't make a fuss
when I said I wanted to go
to culinary school instead
of law school.

contents

breakfast & brunch

soups & salads

sandwiches

pasta & pizza

chicken dinners

the other meats

seafood & vegetarian

party snacks

desserts & cocktails

BLESSED

foreword

First and foremost, I am a huge fan of Shay Spence. We met years ago, during his time as a food editor at *People*. Shay did a cover story about me, my cooking show, and my career. We had the best time during his visit at our ranch in Oklahoma, and by the time he left, I felt like I'd made a lifelong friend. The *People* story was a great memory (and milestone!) for me, but today it makes me chuckle (and makes me so darn happy) to think about how full-circle Shay and I have come. Little did either of us know back then that I—the subject of his magazine profile—would one day consider him—the writer of the profile—to be one of the very best cooking personalities in the country. And I absolutely do!

When Shay left his magazine job to tackle food content full time, I followed his journey online. As an old-time food blogger who experienced firsthand the metamorphosis of social media and algorithm-based food content, I very quickly realized Shay was onto something special and unique with his platform. Whether he was recreating viral recipes, highlighting his favorite (and not-so-favorite!) foods at Disney World, or whipping up a quick skillet dinner in his Key West kitchen on a weeknight, Shay brought such a smart, laid-back, life-loving energy to everything he shared. He brought delicious food, fun vibes, and a genuine sense of "check out this amazing thing I just ate" or "come watch what I'm cooking for dinner" to viewers around the world.

Make no mistake: Shay's grasp of good food is absolutely undeniable, and it's all grounded in instinct, curiosity, and approachability. By his own admission, he didn't grow up cooking or mastering classic techniques. Instead, he learned the way most of us home cooks do—by eating, tasting, trying, watching, failing, and succeeding day in and day out. What I think is so cool about Shay is the combination of perspectives he brings to the table. On one hand, he's lived in New York City, worked with amazing chefs, and has a sharp, sophisticated palate. On the other hand, he grew up in Texas surrounded by barbecue and understands that most home cooks don't use the word "palate." They just want to know what to make for breakfast this morning or dinner tonight. Not for a big party next week or a special occasion next month. They want great food that's delicious, unfussy, and doable, and they want to be able to make it *now*.

Enter Shay's glorious new cookbook! *Meals You Can't Mess Up* is a celebration of everything Shay is about. It includes the types of dishes that have shaped him—and gives readers a little peek into his life as well. On a superficial note, you probably noticed right away the bright colors and unapologetically fun (*ka-POW!*) design of the book, which feels like such a refreshing departure from the serene, neutral world we often see on social media. While this vibrant color scheme will make you smile, the food inside will make your day, week, month, and beyond.

The recipes in this book strike a beautiful balance of being both approachable and extraordinary. Shay has an incredible knack for embracing traditional favorites while also giving them fresh, unexpected spins that make you do a double take in the best way. Mac and cheese with herby dressing? (I have to make this now.) Stuffed bell peppers, but unstuffed in casserole form? (Why have I not thought of this?) Nachos baked in a springform pan? Key lime pie, but make it tiramisu? I could go on and on. These ideas feel brilliantly obvious once you see them—but that's how Shay's food mind works. And the best part is that while the twists are creative and exciting, they never push the dishes out of the realm of familiar, family-friendly favorites.

I don't know how he does it, but Shay can take something as humble and basic as a bologna sandwich and somehow make you want it immediately (and he does, on page 90). He truly understands flavor, texture, and what people actually crave. The pasta dishes in this book are especially at the top of my must-try list of dishes. I love noodles in every form and I got stuck in this section for a solid hour, which reminds me of something I meant to mention earlier: *do not read this cookbook if you're hungry!*

Another thing that shines so clearly throughout this book is the way Shay organizes and designates each recipe. Small tags let you know if a dish takes 30-ish minutes, if it requires no chopping, or if it only takes one pan to make it, and so on. I find these signposts to be invaluable for those times you're thumbing through a cookbook wondering which recipe is going to be the right one. Shay understands that time and energy are just as important as flavor and texture, and he builds this understanding into every recipe he shares here.

This cookbook is absolutely perfect in that it isn't about perfection. It's about opening your fridge and knowing that everything is gonna be just fine. I'm so proud of Shay and thrilled that this book is being launched into the world. I predict it will live on kitchen counters, become splattered with sauce, get dog-eared on favorite pages, and become your new best friend. I plan on enjoying every page and every bite!

Love,
Ree

introduction

It's a tale as old as time: You buy all the ingredients for that "quick-and-easy dinner" that actually took an hour and a half because you had to scrub, peel, slice, and dice three pounds of potatoes, which took you twenty minutes instead of the five minutes of prep time the recipe promised... and you haven't even started cooking yet. Or you spent twenty-two dollars on three different bundles of fresh herbs, only to use a teaspoon of each, knowing you're leaving the rest to rot in the fridge. And maybe after all that heartache, you spent an hour in the kitchen scrubbing four different pots and pans.

This cookbook won't hurt you like that.

As someone who has spent over a decade as a food writer and editor, I've encountered a lot of not-so-great recipes from great chefs. The truth is, cooking for a restaurant kitchen requires primal instinct, adjustments on the fly, and a ferocious speed that simply doesn't always translate to instructing a home cook—and most of us don't have a dedicated team of dishwashers.

When I competed on the second season of Gordon Ramsay's *Next Level Chef*, I learned that I'm kind of the opposite: I can create a damn good recipe for a weeknight dinner, but high-pressure kitchen environments are not my vibe. The running joke on the show was that I was always on "Key West Time," a nod to the fact that I live in the Florida Keys and cook with the sense of urgency of all the manatees that putter around our marinas.

While this aspect of my personality doesn't work on a timed cooking competition judged by the most famous chef in the world, it's allowed me to be more thoughtful in creating actually easy, radically simplified recipes that anyone can make (yes, even those of you who are historically kitchen-challenged and received this book as a gag gift because of the title . . . I see you).

My career has also required me to skim through no fewer than twenty thousand of these cookbook introductions, so I know it's tempting to skip right past these sections and get to the good stuff. There are only so many times one can read about the smell wafting through a stranger's grandmother's kitchen and how their family likes to eat food. I'll try to spare you those details.

But since this is a physical cookbook you've invested in and not a search result or a social media algorithm ambush, I'll assume you have some interest in who I am and why you should take cooking advice from me. So before we get into the recipes, as Hilary Duff sings in her timeless smash hit "Come Clean": "Let's go back, back to the beginning . . ."

who's shay spence, anyway?

My path to becoming a cookbook author was an unlikely one. I did not grow up with even a passing curiosity about how food was made, despite my parents' best efforts. That slow-simmered, cinnamon-spiced Lebanese beef stew my mom was hovering over all day? Fine, I'd eat it, but not before begging for a foot-long Chili Cheese Coney from Sonic first.

While I love my family, I was never super hyped to gather around the dinner table with them; I was instead counting down the seconds and obligatory bites until I could be excused to watch old episodes of *The Munsters* on Nick at Nite. Television was where I got my kicks, and ironically that was my gateway drug to the world of cooking: through the Food Network.

This channel was a feast for all my senses, a treasure trove of various worlds I could step into that felt completely foreign to my life in Texas. I learned there is a real place called the Hamptons, and there's a fabulous woman named Ina Garten who lives there. She taught me that there's such a thing as "good vanilla extract," which confused me because I thought vanilla existed only as ice cream, never considering anything had to be extracted.

From there, I discovered food blogs and got my daily updates from The Pioneer Woman—Ree Drummond—as she showed gorgeous step-by-step photographs of how to make chicken pot pie while musing about the wonders of raising a family of cattle ranchers in Oklahoma. You know, typical fifteen-year-old boy stuff.

After canceling plans to go to law school in favor of culinary school, I landed the dream job for anyone who grew up obsessed with cooking shows: working for Rachael Ray, testing the famous 30-Minute Meals that went into her magazine. This taught me that Rachael operates in an alternate time-space continuum than many of us do, and her minutes are not the same as my minutes (see my previous note about Key West Time). It's a testament to her skill as a speedy cook but also gets to the heart of something I know is a major frustration for home cooks: the timing of it all, and how putting a meal together actually varies from person to person (but more on that in the next chapter).

A couple of years later, I joined *People* magazine as the food editor, developing recipes and writing in-depth articles about the minute differences between each Kardashian's salad order. You may be thinking, *I didn't know* People *has a food section,* which is understandable, as it's usually nestled in the back of the magazine between the profile of a serial killer's mom and the Celebrity Puzzler. As a culinary-school graduate who has seen every episode of every *Real Housewives* franchise (even Dallas), it turned out to be a dream job that I never knew existed.

I got to travel to Pawhuska, Oklahoma, to write stories about the aforementioned Pioneer Woman, who turned her small town into a tourist hub by creating a major empire that all started from a food blog. I made the pilgrimage to Ina Garten's hydrangea-lined house in the Hamptons, too, then subsequently was invited to interview her on two of her book tours.

Having this job and learning from the most successful people in the business taught me the best skill I could ever acquire as a recipe developer: brevity.

Publishing recipes for an audience that was primarily there to read about reality-TV gossip meant that we had to keep it simple. Never more than ten ingredients and as few steps as possible to fit on one page of magazine real estate. If Gordon Ramsay sent in a recipe for Beef Wellington, for example, I'd have to trim the fat (I know there is no fat to be trimmed from the cut of beef used for a Wellington, and I wouldn't dare touch Ramsay's most famous recipe, so perhaps that's not the best example . . . but you get the idea).

So how do I take this expert's amazing dish, remove some ingredients, combine some steps, and get rid of a pan or two so that it's actually easy and a crowd pleaser for home cooks without annihilating the integrity of the original dish? That's another stepping stone in how this book came to be, because I develop my recipes with that perspective in mind.

Blue
BAY

my path to minor internet stardom

I started posting cooking videos on Instagram in 2018, when the fickle social media algorithms had overtaken the Food Network's decades-long domination of recipe content. At a certain point, it began to feel like a true race to the bottom, prioritizing page-view counts and engagement at the expense of providing useful service to home cooks. If you do something wrong, pronounce something incorrectly on purpose, or create some piece of outrageous stunt food, people will comment and share it, and boom—your video goes out to millions more people, and acts of kitchen malpractice spread like wildfire. These days, we call this "rage-bait."

My first viral moment is a perfect example, though I like to think I'm the hero of this tale. There was a thing called the "pizzadilla" making its rounds on what was then known as Twitter. It started with a video created by one of the many cursed, bootleg offsprings of Buzzfeed's "Tasty" series, and the recipe involved spice-rubbing chicken breasts; baking and shredding them; tossing them with barbecue sauce; layering it between mounds of cheese and tortillas in a springform pan; freezing it; cutting it into wedges; breading each wedge with flour, egg, then breadcrumbs; deep-frying each wedge; putting them back together in the shape of a pizza; topping with marinara sauce, cheese, and pepperoni; then baking it all until the cheese melted. This monstrous creation was then served with a homemade ranch dressing on the side. (The algorithm trick here was that you never knew what was coming next—a longer watch time means more viewers.)

As a drastically impulsive glutton for punishment, I thought it would be funny to recreate the recipe on my Instagram stories. I documented every grueling step as the color slowly faded from my face in the wee hours of the morning. Around midnight, my friend texted me that my pizzadilla journey had been retweeted by Chrissy Teigen and a few other Twitter notables. Suddenly, I had tens of thousands of viewers from all over the world cheering me on in real time. I woke up the next day to eighteen thousand Instagram followers, an article written about me in the *New York Post*, and a request to go on the *Today* show, which I had to politely decline in order to hop on a flight to Disney World to cover the opening of Star Wars: Galaxy's Edge.

Now I treat my social channels like my own little chaotic television show, with the content of each episode dictated by my whims of the day. I mix in breezy recipe tutorials from my island kitchen in Key West with wackier and wilder culinary adventures like rating every key lime pie in the Florida Keys, eating my way through all two-hundred-plus restaurants at Disney World, finding the best onion rings on the Las Vegas Strip, and traveling across the globe to Chongqing, China, to visit the world's largest hot-pot restaurant . . . just to name a few.

But there is a throughline to all of it: the desire to create a sense of approachability and fun without the pretension you often find in the culinary field. In the introduction to her first cookbook, Ina Garten said that "food is not about impressing people... it's about making them feel comfortable," and this is a philosophy that has stuck with me.

In this book, you'll find recipes for personal comfort foods, from dishes that have been in my family for decades (Mom's Mujadara, a Lebanese dish, page 192; my dad's Tex-Mex, salsa-braised Carne Guisada, page 175), ones inspired by my husband James' Milwaukee upbringing (Hard Cider–Braised Brats, page 155), street foods we've enjoyed during our travels together (Honeymoon Choripán, page 89), and some that celebrate the island life we've created in Key West (Key Lime Shrimp Rolls, Two Ways, page 78). You'll also find plenty of dishes that I have no cultural connection to but that are universally comforting, like my Laze-agna (page 110).

I've grown my social media presence to over two million followers by sharing recipes that are basically the opposite of everything the pizzadilla represented: radically simplified meals that maximize flavor using minimal ingredients, time, and dishes. In short, the kind of recipes you can't mess up.

the meals you can't mess up mindset

To come up with dishes that are actually foolproof, I considered what my social media followers identified as their greatest pain points. The biggest hurdles are when recipes take longer than estimated, require too many expensive ingredients, leave a mess and lots of dirty dishes behind, or require exhausting prep work.

That's why no recipe in this book calls for more than ten ingredients (minus the freebie items I mention on the next page). Over half of these meals can be prepared in one pot or pan (and never more than two). Most come together in thirty or so minutes, and many require zero chopping or slicing. Now, I know it's not exactly groundbreaking to come up with a thirty-minute meal as a hook (did I mention I worked for Rachael Ray?), but it's a hit concept for a reason!

30ish minutes

30ish-minute recipes

I kind of hate to list cooking times. Not only does everyone chop, dice, and slice at different rates, but there are countless variables, from altitude to equipment, that come into play and affect how long one cook's process might take compared with another. Gas stoves heat pans faster than electric, and nonstick pans heat faster than cast-iron skillets. Heat levels even vary between different burners on the same stove! Consider the cook and prep times as general estimations, give or take five to ten minutes. When in doubt, rely on visual and other sensory indicators mentioned in recipe directions. Most of the recipes in this category will take you less than thirty minutes!

one dish

one-dish recipes

I firmly believe the number-one reason people don't like cooking is due to the looming dread of postmeal cleanup. But one-dish recipes can be tricky in their own right. For example, I've messed up a lot of one-pot pastas in my life because everything turned into a gloopy, starchy mess. In developing one-pot pastas, I've taken into account the best shapes for the right recipes. In my One-Pot Pancetta, Kale, and Mushroom Orecchiette (page 114), I've perfected the liquid-to-pasta ratio to the best of my ability, but it's important to be able to adjust on the fly, as different brands of pasta will differ in sturdiness and starchiness—more on pasta cooking on page 24!

The same goes for sheet-pan meals or one-pot braises, since a whole chicken thigh is not going to cook at the same rate as, say, a slice of bell pepper. If you're not strategic, part of the dish might burn or get soggy, while the other elements stay undercooked. That's why all my sheet-pan meals in this book consist of ingredients with the same cooking time (Orange-Miso Salmon with Broccolini, page 186; James' Favorite Parmesan Pork Chops, page 152). The truth is, each dish requires its own special tweaks and methods to make it perfect. The good part is I've already done that work for you!

6 ingredients

6-ingredient recipes

These recipes include six ingredients or less. Keep in mind that there are six freebie ingredients I'll always assume you have on hand that don't count toward the total number of ingredients required: a neutral cooking oil or cooking spray (I'm partial to avocado or an extra-light olive oil) that can withstand high heat for searing and sautéing, a good-quality extra-virgin olive oil for salad dressings and for finishing, butter (which I always have on hand) for lower-heat sautéing or giving a silky finish to a dish, and then, of course, salt and pepper. This may be more controversial, but I also include crushed red pepper flakes as a freebie ingredient—this is just as much of a household staple as black pepper for me, and I have a whole drawer full of red pepper packets I've collected from pizza delivery spots.

I originally wanted to go with the more common "Five-Ingredient Recipes" for this category, but I actually found it constricting and almost always hit a wall when the dish begged for a sixth component. Author Samin Nosrat famously outlined salt, fat, acid, and heat as the main pillars foundational to cooking; beyond that, we need starches, fresh herbs, warm spices, and occasional umami elements to make a dish pop and feel complete.

I know grocery trips are expensive, so rest assured that every ingredient included in a recipe will be instrumental to the final product. With regard to fresh herbs in particular, I like to stick to one per dish and let that flavor really shine—unless you're making Thanksgiving stuffing (or my Tabbouleh with Spiced Chickpeas, page 193, where the herbs act as the lettuce for the salad). You'll notice that whenever there is an abundance of any leftover ingredient, whether it's fresh parsley or an open can of chipotle peppers in adobo, I'll always give you a practical way to use what's left behind (my Green Godd-ish dressing, page 73, uses up an abundance of fresh herbs!) or direct you to another recipe that puts them to good use.

no chop

no-chop recipes

I may love these recipes the most—not only because I had the worst knife skills in my culinary-school class, but because I rarely come across no-chop recipes. Yet there are so many meals I make on a regular basis that don't require me to pull out a cutting board! With my Burst Tomato-Basil Tortellini (page 94), you simply cook the whole cherry tomatoes until they start to pop open and create a sauce, roughly tear in some fresh basil leaves with your hands so they start to release flavorful oils, then finish with creamy burrata.

It's often said that clean hands are a cook's best tool, but I'd add that they're the most underutilized tool. I almost never actually chop fresh greens. I'd rather tear them into bite-size pieces for salads or in braises. Even for something like my Bourbon Blueberry French Toast Casserole (page 40), I tear the bread instead of dicing, which turns out more rustic and gorgeous.

I'm also not above buying pre-prepped ingredients from the grocery store, like chopped onions, matchstick carrots, or sliced mushrooms. You generally pay a premium, but these time-saving items make quick weeknight meals come together even faster. The quality diminishment is negligible, particularly when the ingredients are being cooked down anyway, like the carrots in my Thai Basil Red Curry (page 181). My one major exception is jarred chopped garlic, which you can read about in my essential ingredients section on page 27.

One day, I'll write a cookbook of all no-chop recipes, but for now, we've got a really stellar start. These dishes were the most popular among my recipe testers for this book. And on that note, let's talk about . . .

the testing process

I diligently cooked through all the recipe in this book multiple times to make sure they were perfect in my kitchen, but it was really important to me that we live up to the title of *Meals You Can't Mess Up* . . . no matter who you are. That means making sure they will work across various ovens, equipment, ingredient brands, and kitchen skill levels.

In addition to hiring recipe testers with culinary-industry credentials, I also enlisted friends and loved ones with a wide variety of cooking backgrounds—including my lovely husband, who literally only knows how to cook bratwursts (but he's damn good at that, okay? He also makes a perfect vodka soda with lemon, and I love him).

This process was designed to identify obstacles for the most novice of cooks. While I don't consider this to be strictly a beginner's cookbook, I want to provide every detail that is necessary for success, along with tips on how you can course-correct quickly if, for some reason, things start to go south.

Through this rigorous crowdsourcing, I learned a lot that I wouldn't have from a professional recipe tester. Some people were confused by the use of the word "divided" after an ingredient on the recipe list. This is a common cookbook term that means you use the same ingredient in separate parts at different stages of the recipe. For example, "3 tbsp butter, divided" simply means that you may use two tablespoons of the butter at the beginning of the recipe to sauté the vegetables, then a final tablespoon to stir into the dish at the end. It never occurred to me that I might need to explain that further to a home cook, who may not be familiar with the jargon.

Other feedback involved minorly tragic errors. One tester used cured Spanish chorizo instead of fresh chorizo for the Honeymoon Choripán sandwich (page 89), which leads to a dry, chewy, salty disaster. There were more serious safety hazards, too. One friend suffered oil-splatter burns while making the Weeknight Carnitas-Style Chicken Tacos (page 133), which has now been revised to prevent the same from happening to you. (Everyone, say thank you to Jessica.)

You'll find all these potential red flags and how to avoid them on each recipe page, so this book should really be called *Meals You Can't Mess Up (with My Help . . . and the Sacrifices of My Loved Ones)*.

Go for the Gusto

Lovely day for a GUINNESS

how to mess up a meal

When I say "mess up" a meal in this context, I mean render it fully inedible. There are certain times when you really hit a point of no return and you either have to leave the dish out for the raccoons or suffer through it and take the hit to your ego. I never want you to face this dilemma, so here are the most common, unfixable mistakes.

oversalting

Professional chefs and cooks have notoriously salt-driven palates (myself included), and one thing I've learned from being married to a man who has a much more sensitive disposition is to rein it in. When I first started cooking, I was instructed to salt the pasta water "like the sea." Doing so flavors the pasta itself and leaves you with starchy water that helps bring a pasta sauce together during the final steps. If you've ever tasted a mouthful of ocean water, you know that it's probably not something you'd ever want to add to your food, and taking this advice too literally has resulted in many inedible pans of otherwise beautiful pasta during my cooking career. My rule now is to use no more than three large pinches of salt per pot of pasta water, which is about 1½ teaspoons—but who's measuring, anyway?

Truthfully, I don't typically like to give measurements for salt because I find it's a very personal journey even within each household, and different types and brands of salt bear different levels of saltiness. When I do give salt measurements, it's to guide you in the right direction . . . but feel free to take it with a grain of salt and season to your liking.

Just remember: You can't ruin a dish by undersalting, but once you've gone too far, it's nearly impossible to come back from. So my guidance is to start conservatively by adding small amounts, and build up to what you know works for you. Taste as you go and remember that you need just enough to make the flavors pop for your palate. When in doubt, finish the dish with a bit of fancy flaky salt, and say that's what you meant to do all along.

burning

There are obvious ways to burn an entire dish, like leaving it in the oven or under the broiler for too long. Those are tough to recover from but are easily preventable with a timer. What I'm more concerned about are stealthier burnt ingredients that you might not notice until you dig into dinner. The most common culprit is garlic.

In a particularly cursed episode of *Sex and the City*, Big is cooking pasta sauce for Carrie and tries to make a metaphor about why he won't marry her yet. "It's all in the timing," he says. "You've gotta brown the garlic before you put in the onions." Of all the asinine trash that man did and said on that show, this was his biggest offense. Under no circumstances should you be browning garlic, and it should never go in before the onions. Browned garlic is two seconds away from burnt garlic, and burnt garlic permeates the whole dish with an acrid flavor that lingers unpleasantly, much like Big during the entire *Sex and the City* series. I always sauté garlic for about thirty seconds tops (even if a recipe says longer), and in some instances, you want it merely to kiss the pan, to barely cook for about ten seconds, like in my French Onion Steak Bites (page 168) and the Sizzling Garlic Shrimp a la Schiller's (page 210).

undercooking

During my early days of culinary school, I somehow ended up at a stranger's rooftop on the Fourth of July in New York City. By default, I was tasked with grilling chicken for the whole party. I got beautiful grill marks all over the drumsticks, sauced them up, and garnished them, and everyone chowed down on that wonderful char, which gave way to a revolting pink, raw center.

Sure, I was able to salvage the chicken by simply throwing it all back on the grill, but I was never able to recover my reputation, nor was I willing to show my face in front of that crowd again. But, thankfully, no salmonella outbreaks were reported in the area afterward, to my knowledge.

I know that undercooking meat, especially chicken, is a major fear for home cooks. I also know that for many of us scatterbrains, using a meat thermometer—while helpful—feels impractical and tedious, and we would much rather just go on vibes. To this day, when I am cooking chicken, I choose the thickest of the bunch for myself. Not because I'm greedy. If the thickest piece is cooked through, you can be confident you're good.

overcooking

When it comes to expensive cuts of meat that aren't steak, I'm not as concerned about overcooking, particularly in the forgiving recipes I created for this book.

The key is to go with a protein that is more conducive to longer cook times—like chicken thighs over breasts, as they have more fat and stay juicy well after they're cooked through, as seen in the Grilled Tuscan-esque Chicken (page 146) or the Braised Chicken with Italian Beans and Greens (page 142).

Even with chicken breasts and leaner cuts of meat, overcooking is salvageable! My secret is to go saucier, like with my Skillet Raclette Chicken, which sits in a creamy leek-and-mushroom sauce (page 134) or the Thai Basil Red Curry with Snapper (page 181). And if you're ever worried about overcooking meat on the grill, where there's less control over the heat level, keep a flavorful sauce on hand that can go on everything in a pinch. I recommend my Calabrian chili chimichurri sauce that's paired with the Honeymoon Choripán (page 89); it's one of those rare condiments that is amazing on steak, chicken, fish, and pork. Slice the meat to increase sauce-to-surface area, and most people won't even notice it's overcooked. (Serving cocktails helps, too, if you're into that.)

I have a lot of shrimp recipes in this book because they're an essential component of the Key West lifestyle and are a perfect protein for fast weeknight meals. You definitely don't want to overcook shrimp. They become rubbery and chewy in a way no sauce can cover up. That's why I pull them from the pan as soon as they start to change color (we're talking one to two minutes per side). If the recipe calls for a sauce, like with the Homecomin' Shrimp and White Cheddar Grits (page 54), submerge them and gently warm through, right before serving.

oven and stovetop errors and variations

My oven is different from your oven, and my stovetop is different from your stovetop. There's no way around this.

To get an accurate reading of the temperature inside your oven, I recommend buying an oven thermometer. They're cheap and easy; you simply hang it on one of the racks.

I don't expect the average cook to do this, because I don't when I'm not testing recipes for public consumption! The important thing is that you get to know your oven and how it ticks. You can do that by periodically checking on your dish as it cooks to look for visual indicators. This is, of course, harder to do with, say, a Thanksgiving turkey, but for any of the casseroles or easy bakes in this book, you'll know when something is brown and bubbly. Eventually, you will be able to tell the hot spots in your oven for all future references too. And rotating the pan periodically is always a good idea no matter what you're cooking.

Stoves also vary. One good thing to know is which burner to use and when. Almost all stovetops have larger and smaller burners. In general, I steer clear of the smaller burners unless I'm gently heating a sauce or soup in a small pan. The larger burners have a wider flame and will heat your pan faster and more evenly, resulting in a more successful execution of any dish.

breaking rules and busting myths

I wrote earlier about online cooks purposely using totally whack techniques as engagement bait for algorithm manipulation, but I've found a work-around that maintains my integrity: unconventional, sometimes controversial methods that actually work and make your life easier. Here are just a few examples, and you'll find more on the recipe pages.

starting pasta in cold water

The easiest way to rile up a mob of angry Italians in your comments section is to throw pasta straight into a little pot, cover it with cold water, and get cooking. Traditionally, you bring water to a rapid, rolling boil before you even think about dropping one little noodle in the pot.

I've been cooking pasta from cold water out of pure laziness since college. It turns out, I'm vindicated by science. Alton Brown, star of the Food Network's *Good Eats* and food-scientist extraordinaire, conducted experiments on his website and concluded that starting with a smaller amount of cold water and the pasta immediately in the water is a superior method that creates a concentrated, starchier water ideal for thickening and emulsifying your pasta sauce.

marinating: what is it good for?

One of the first cooking techniques I learned was to toss some chicken breasts in a bottle of Italian salad dressing and let it sit overnight before cooking. I've evolved a lot in my culinary journey since then, but I'm still not a huge fan of marination. So much of that liquid gets wasted, which goes against my rule of maximum flavor with minimal ingredients. I prefer to impart flavor in smaller amounts toward the end of the cooking process, by including a luscious sauce or compound butter, as is the case in my Shortcut Shrimp Scampi Risotto (page 185), where a lemon-garlic butter is stirred in for an ultra-rich finishing touch that suffuses the dish. For the Athenian Chicken (page 138), marination takes only a short amount of time. The sauce comes together super quick, and I always save a little of the marinade to brush on at the end to perk it up.

baking with salted butter

Okay, I don't totally have the science to back this one up, mostly vibes. While conventional wisdom is to use unsalted butter in baked goods to control the salt level, I've simply always baked with salted butter. I don't bake a ton, so when I do, I'm gonna use what I have on hand, and that's salted butter. In my opinion, it just tastes better. And you know what? I find I prefer my baked goods on the saltier side. It's not just me, either. Cookbook author Justine Doiron (who is a much better baker than I am) also sings the praises of salted-butter baked goods, calling it "flavor insurance." So when I call for butter in this book, it's always salted—even in desserts, like the super buttery Mixed-Berry Cardamom Cobbler (page 230).

washing mushrooms

One of the most heinous myths I grew up thinking was true was that you can't wash mushrooms because they'll get waterlogged and soggy before you even cook them. Again, Alton Brown came to the rescue and debunked this. Not only can you wash mushrooms with no quality deterioration, but I would go one step further and posit that it's crucial! I make sure my shrooms are thoroughly rinsed of dirt and grit, then patted dry so they can brown while cooking, which you can then use in dishes like the Spinach and Mushroom Sheet-Pan Pizzadillas (page 124)—a much-improved version of the previously mentioned pizzadilla I made that took the internet by storm.

the bare (kitchen) necessities

A well-stocked kitchen of essential ingredients and tools is the best way to cut down on weekly grocery bills and to make your life easier when you're planning what to cook. Here are a few that you'll find often repeated in this book (and why), plus all the specialty equipment you'll need to make any of the recipes.

staple ingredients

salt

There are so many opinions out there when it comes to salt, and way too many options to choose from, though almost all chefs will tell you to go with kosher salt. Diamond Crystal is the preferred industry standard, because it's got a nice coarseness that isn't as harshly salty as Morton's kosher salt, the standard competitor. I actually prefer using fine kosher salt (also available from Diamond Crystal) because it dissolves faster, which is especially useful when adjusting seasoning at the end of a dish.

oils

You'll often find my recipes call for a neutral oil, which is any cooking oil that can withstand high temperatures and has no noticeable flavor. I hate canola oil because to me, it's not neutral at all and has a distinctly fishy odor. My go-to is avocado oil or extra-light olive oil, although if I'm feeling less spendy or using a lot of oil for frying, I'll opt for peanut oil or a no-frills vegetable oil.

calabrian chili paste (or chopped calabrian chilis)

This used to be an ingredient you'd only find at ultra-specific Italian specialty markets, but now it's stocked at my little island grocery store, so I know the tide has thankfully turned. Calabrian chili paste has an addictive, tangy, slightly fruity heat that is singular. I love it stirred into pasta sauces, like my Mascarpone Rigatoni alla Vodka (page 102), and it's excellent as a condiment for adding bright heat.

instant mashed potatoes

Instant mashed potatoes are useful for thickening soups and stews. For making actual mashed potatoes, I stick to real spuds, but I put this ingredient into action by using a small amount in my Lemon Chicken Tortellini Soup (page 66) or using a heavier hand in my Charred Corn & Potato Chowder (page 64), where it reinforces the fresh potato flavor in addition to thickening. (Instant mashed potatoes are also a great substitute for breadcrumbs to make a light-and-crispy crust for fish and chicken).

evaporated milk

Evaporated milk is one of my all-time favorites. It's shelf stable so you don't have to worry about it going bad, it has a much lower fat content than heavy cream, and it's a more stable dairy product so it can stand up to heat without breaking as easily. Whenever I want to add creaminess without too much richness, I reach for a can.

passata

Passata, a classic Italian staple, is a smooth puree of uncooked, strained tomatoes that acts as more of a blank canvas upon which to build flavor. I often see passata stocked in grocery stores now, but if you can't find a bottle, you can use pureed tomatoes. I particularly love it in my cinnamon-spiced Lebanese Beef & Green Beans (page 172).

canned or boxed soup

No offense to the good people at Campbell's, but the quality of prepared soup on grocery store shelves has vastly improved in recent years. I keep a few boxes stashed in my pantry so I can doctor up weeknight dinners. By adding a few spices, you can whip up the sauce for my Cheesy Butternut Squash Pasta Bake (page 113) or amp up the Curry Tomato Soup with Chili-Garlic Naan Croutons (page 63).

pre-peeled garlic

I know it's a popular shortcut, but I simply cannot advocate for those jars of minced garlic. To me, one spoonful can easily ruin a dish, but if you like that, keep going, babe. What I can support is pre-peeled whole garlic, which maintains flavor integrity and freshness. This is particularly great when you need a lot of garlic, like, say, twenty cloves for my aromatic 20-Clove Roasted Garlic Pasta al Limone (page 101). The garlic roasts into a sweet paste, so no one will know you didn't tediously peel an entire bulb yourself.

rotisserie chicken

If there is no rotisserie chicken in my refrigerator, then call the police, because I am deceased. I could make a whole cookbook with shredded-rotisserie-chicken recipes (though I'm almost positive someone already has). Some of my favorite ones in this book are my Wasabi Avocado Chicken Salad Toasts (page 86) and my Weeknight Carnitas-Style Chicken Tacos (page 133).

marinated cheese

I can almost never pass up a tub of marinated mozzarella balls or, even better, marinated feta cubes. Not just because they are delicious for snacking, but because they are a double-duty ingredient. Toss the cheese into salads, then use the oil (which is generally flavored with garlic, peppers, and herbs) to make the dressing in my Lamb Chops with Feta & Mint Orzo Salad (page 171) or the Kale & Fennel Salad (page 69).

freezer-aisle shortcuts

Sadly, one of my greatest joys in life is strolling through the freezer aisles at my local Publix. Some of my most popular shortcut recipes have come about from these blissful walks! I use frozen tater tots in the Chicken Chili Tot Pie (page 145) or the Sweet Potato & Asparagus Fri-tot-a (page 47). Frozen fire-roasted corn also comes in handy to add a smoky flavor without having to grill corn yourself, like in my Chili-Lime Corn & Black Bean Tacos (page 197). I love frozen bread dough to make my Dollywood-Style Cinnamon Bread (page 53), which comes out better than any time I've tried to make the bread from scratch. There are many more freezer-aisle hidden gems in the pages that follow.

gear and gadgets

12-inch (30cm) oven-safe sauté pan

A large, oven-safe sauté pan is the most essential piece of equipment for making my recipes and something every home cook should own, whether you're making a casserole, a one-pot pasta, or a skillet-pan pizza (page 118). They're great because you can go from browning something on the stovetop when you need high heat to popping it straight into the oven to finish cooking. I prefer sauté pans to skillets because they have straight sides as opposed to sloped sides to keep everything in there, and a 12-inch (30cm) is better than a 10-inch (25cm) if you're cooking for at least four people. Of course, a well-seasoned cast-iron skillet is always a good alternative, but I prefer a ceramic nonstick style, like Caraway, which requires much less upkeep and is easier to clean.

food processor

I don't whip out a food processor unless it's absolutely necessary, but using this machine does come in handy from time to time. Any model will do, though there are benefits to owning a smaller one (3.5 cups) for making things like salad dressings in addition to a large one (10 to 12 cups) for heftier tasks, like making my Whipped Ricotta Dip with Pistachio-Artichoke Pesto (page 206). They're also great for shredding a whole block of Parmesan cheese in an instant, which will give you so much more flavor than the pre-grated stuff.

hand mixer

I do own a fancy, expensive KitchenAid stand mixer, but it stays locked away in a cupboard like Harry Potter because I don't bake enough to justify owning it! Instead, I always reach for my cheap little electric hand mixer to get minor whipping tasks done, like the mascarpone frosting for my Key Lime Tiramisu (page 237).

rasp or microplane

Microplane is a brand of narrow metal graters. Necessary for any kitchen, a Microplane yields the fluffiest grated cheese to finish a dish, and it easily turns a clove of garlic into a fine paste (which is what I mean when I call for "grated" garlic in a recipe). It's the only tool I use to zest lemons, limes, and oranges—which I call for often to add more citrus flavor without extra acidity. You can use one to freshly grate nutmeg for the Frozen Key Lime Painkillers (page 242), too. You can find cheaper rasp-style alternatives, but it's worth investing in the real deal because they last for years and the sturdy handle provides a safer, more comfortable experience.

bench scraper

If you don't like making a mess while transferring a bunch of chopped vegetables to a pan or a bowl, a bench scraper is your ticket to happiness. The flat, square piece of metal means you can scoop up veggies in a clean and dignified fashion while preventing spillage.

muffin tins

This may seem like a random addition, as you'll notice I don't have any muffin recipes in this book. In fact, I don't think I've ever baked muffins. But if you follow me on socials, you know I have worn out my muffin tins. I use the standard 12-cup tins to make fun savory snacks with crispy golden edges, like my Muffin-Tin Pepperoni-Jalapeño Pizza Rolls (page 127). I also keep a 24-cup mini muffin tin around for more bite-size snacks, like my Cheeseburger Wontons (page 227).

relaxing (or ignoring) the rules

I know I've laid out a lot in these introductory chapters, and it's a lot to take in. While I believe breaking certain rules is crucial to easier cooking, I'm now giving you permission to relax the rules in general.

My goal here is to get you comfortable in the kitchen, or maybe learn some new tricks if you are already comfortable. Nothing about cooking is cut and dried. It's all based on personal palates and experiences, and like with anything, you get better with time.

There's a reason I moved from New York City to be on Key West Time. This island is a calming place for me, and as an anxious person, calm is not my default setting. The kitchen has always been another calming place for me (which is maybe why, spoiler alert, I didn't win that show).

Hopefully, if you make your way through these recipes, you can find that calming feeling in the kitchen, too. And if you don't—well, at least you'll know some super quick and delicious meals you can make to get you the hell out of there as soon as possible.

Enjoy the food, my friends!

breakfast & brunch

30ish minutes

6 ingredients

no chop

one dish

perfect scrambled eggs
(aka hotel eggs)

prep time
5 minutes

cook time
5 minutes

yield
serves 4

8 eggs
1 tsp kosher salt
3 tbsp salted butter, divided
Freshly ground black pepper, to serve
Minced chives, to serve (optional)

As someone who travels and eats for a living, there's one constant that's always there for me no matter where I am—room-service scrambled eggs, preferably eaten late at night. Hotel eggs have the perfect scrambled texture: large curds gently folded into a sturdy (but not browned) exterior that gives way to a softer (but not runny) center. I've mastered the art of making these at home with a few important tricks.

Aggressively whisking the eggs will create small, frothy air bubbles that will ensure fluffiness. Your pan should start really hot so the edges immediately firm up, then keep the heat low. Gently folding—don't stir!—with a silicone spatula will form the large curds. Finishing with a little pat of butter is an insurance policy, in case you happen to overcook the scramble.

1. To a large bowl, add the eggs and salt. Whisk vigorously for at least 1 minute, until completely uniform in color and small bubbles form at the surface.
2. To a medium nonstick skillet over medium-high heat, add 2 tablespoons of the butter and cook for 2 minutes, until it just starts to foam, then reduce the heat to medium-low.
3. Give the eggs another strong whisk and add them to the pan. Let sit for 20 seconds, then run a silicone spatula around the edges of the skillet and gently fold sections toward the center of the pan three or four times to create large curds. Let sit for another 20 seconds, then gently fold around the edges again.
4. Remove from the heat and add the remaining tablespoon butter to the center, then fold the edges over the center one more time. Serve immediately, topped with the black pepper and chives, if using.

bust a myth

Chefs used to always say not to salt eggs ahead of time because it makes them tough, but recent side-by-side tests from J. Kenji López-Alt (among other food scientists) have proven the exact opposite—salting your eggs 5 to 10 minutes ahead of time yields fluffier results, and makes sure they are evenly seasoned.

don't mess it up!

The easiest way to mess up scrambled eggs is to overcook them until they are dry and spongy, which can happen in an instant. Though I really don't like my scrambled eggs wet at all, I turn off the heat while they are still a little bit liquidy on top. The carryover cooking in the time before you serve them will make sure they have a perfect firm-but-not-dry consistency.

30ish minutes

6 ingredients

one dish

pizza eggs

They say necessity is the mother of invention, and that's how the legend of Pizza Eggs begins. My college roommates introduced me to this delicacy when all we had in the refrigerator was leftover pizza and eggs, and it has been an ever-present force in my life for the last fifteen years. The key to perfect pizza eggs is not to rush the process: The pizza needs to get deeply, uniformly caramelized—especially the cheesy parts—before you add the eggs so the little croutons can maintain their crunch while contrasting with the soft scramble. I promised all my loved ones I would include Pizza Eggs in this cookbook. You're welcome!

prep time
5 minutes

cook time
10 minutes

yield
serves 4

- 8 eggs
- Kosher salt, to taste
- 2 tbsp olive oil
- 2 slices of leftover pizza, cut into bite-size pieces
- Fresh basil, to serve (optional)
- Hot sauce or chili oil, to serve (optional)

1. To a large bowl, add the eggs and a pinch of salt. Whisk vigorously for at least 1 minute, until they are completely uniform in color and small bubbles form at the surface.
2. To a large nonstick skillet over medium-high heat, add the oil and heat for 1 minute, or until shimmering. Add the pizza and cook, stirring frequently, until each piece is crispy all over. Reduce the heat to low.
3. Give the eggs another whisk and add them to the pan. Let sit for 20 seconds, until the eggs start to set around the edges, then use a silicone spatula to gently fold the edges to the center in 2-inch sections, making large curds around the pizza bits. Repeat this folding process one more time, then immediately remove from the heat. If the eggs are still wet in spots, continue to fold the hot edges over to finish cooking to your desired doneness.
4. Serve topped with basil and drizzled with the hot sauce or chili oil, if using.

don't mess it up!

The cheese on the pizza can easily stick to a skillet, particularly a stainless-steel pan, so it's very important to use one with a solid nonstick coating (a well-seasoned cast iron is great for pizza eggs). Be sure to stir the pizza frequently and don't be afraid to add a little more oil before the eggs go in to keep things slick.

30ish minutes

6 ingredients

no chop

one dish

fritos migas breakfast tacos

prep time
5 minutes

cook time
10 minutes

yield
serves 4

8 large eggs
½ cup milk
½ tsp kosher salt
½ tsp freshly ground black pepper
2 tbsp salted butter or oil
2 cups corn chips, preferably Fritos Scoops!
5 slices of American cheese, torn into pieces

to serve
Warm flour tortillas
¼ cup chipotle salsa, preferably Casa Martinez brand
Cilantro leaves (optional)

People always ask me for the best breakfast taco in my hometown of Austin, Texas, but that's like asking what the best Kirsten Dunst movie is . . . The answer is all of them. There is one breakfast taco that arguably does stand above the rest, though: the Spicy Chipotle Migas and Queso Taco from Tamale House East, an institution that's been around since Eisenhower was president. Crunchy tortilla chips get cooked into fluffy scrambled eggs along with smoky chipotle salsa and a creamy queso. Everything gets piled onto a soft flour tortilla that somehow remains sturdy enough not to fold under the pressure. It's the taco equivalent of the Wolf Wall cheerleading pyramid from *Bring It On* (arguably the best Kirsten Dunst movie). When I'm homesick, I make this riff by melting American cheese right into the eggs to mimic the queso and top it with store-bought chipotle salsa (I'm a fan of the Casa Martinez brand). Oh, and I like to use those big Fritos in lieu of tortilla chips because they're a little sturdier and more fun.

1. In a large bowl, whisk the eggs and milk together thoroughly and season with salt and pepper.
2. To a medium skillet over medium heat, add the butter. Then add the egg mixture and the corn chips, gently tossing to ensure all the chips are coated in the egg. Add in the cheese and cook for 4 minutes, stirring gently occasionally, until the eggs are just set and the cheese is melted. Immediately remove from the heat and serve on the warm tortillas with the salsa and cilantro, if using.

use it up!

If you have leftover American cheese, use it for the Cheeseburger Wontons (page 227) or in place of the provolone cheese in the Texas Toast Grilled Cheezies (page 81).

If you have leftover Fritos, use them as a crunch in the Tex-Mex Chopped Salad (page 70).

To use the rest of the jar of salsa, add it to my Choriqueso Enchilada Casserole (page 160) in place of the salsa verde for a smokier twist.

30ish minutes

no chop

one dish

moroccan-style poached eggs
with greens

When I lived in New York City, I went to one place the most for lunch: Cafe Mogador, a sweet little Middle Eastern restaurant in the East Village. I always ordered the Moroccan Eggs, which were perfectly poached in a spiced tomato-and-pepper sauce. I am lousy at poaching eggs in water (very easy to mess up!), so I like to gently cook them right in the sauce, shakshuka-style. At Mogador, you have the option to add lamb merguez sausage, but for this recipe, I decided to throw some Tuscan (or dino) kale into the mix, for our health. It's slightly less bitter than standard curly kale, but any leafy green like spinach, mustard greens, or Swiss chard will do.

prep time
5 minutes

cook time
15 minutes

yield
serves 4

2 tbsp harissa
2 tsp za'atar
2 tsp smoked paprika
2 cups passata
1 cup torn Tuscan kale
Kosher salt and freshly ground black pepper, to taste
6 eggs
Pita, to serve

1 To a large skillet or sauté pan over medium heat on the largest burner of your stove, add the harissa and spices and toast for 15 seconds. Add the passata, kale, and ½ cup water, then season with salt and pepper to taste. Let simmer for 5 minutes, until the kale starts to wilt.

2 In a separate bowl, crack the eggs. Reduce the heat to low. Use a ladle to gently nest the eggs, one at a time, into the sauce. Cover with a lid and let poach until the whites are set, about 6 minutes if you like them runnier and 8 minutes for a more set yolk. Serve with the pita.

don't mess it up!

You could crack the eggs directly in the pan, but I like to crack them in a separate bowl first to make sure each yolk remains intact and that there's no trace of shell in the sauce. I've found a ladle is the most successful tool for gently transferring each egg from the bowl into the sauce without yolk breakage.

And though you should leave the lid on during the poaching process to create steam that facilitates even cooking, check them after about 4 minutes to make sure the eggs are cooking evenly. If you notice some are cooking faster than others, that means they are in a hotter spot on your stovetop and you should rotate or move the pan so the undercooked eggs get more attention. When the whites are no longer translucent but still have some jiggle to them, it's time to turn off the heat!

amp it up

If you want to add some extra flavor to the pita, brush some olive oil over the top and sprinkle with more of the za'atar you use in the dish, then pop it under the broiler on a baking sheet for about a minute or two, until just lightly toasted.

ingredient intel

Harissa is a garlicky, spiced red pepper paste from North Africa that's great mixed in to sauces and dressings or as an accompaniment to meats and seafoods. Swap it out for the sundried tomato pesto in my Grilled Tuscan-esque Chicken (page 146) for a spicy, smoky twist on the dish, or use it in place of sriracha in my Spicy Chicken Caesar Naan Wraps (page 82).

no chop

one dish

bourbon blueberry french toast casserole

prep time
15 minutes, plus chilling time

cook time
55 minutes

yield
serves 8

- 1lb (450g) artisan bread loaf such as sourdough, torn into bite-size pieces
- 1 cup fresh blueberries
- 8 eggs
- 1½ cups half-and-half
- ½ cup plus 1 tbsp sugar, divided
- 3 tbsp bourbon
- 3 tbsp salted butter, melted
- 1¼ tsp ground cinnamon, divided
- Pinch of kosher salt
- 2 tbsp powdered sugar, to serve
- Maple syrup, to serve

One thing you'll never find me doing if I'm cooking breakfast for a crowd is standing over a splattering skillet, flipping pancakes or cooking eggs to order. Y'all can head over to Denny's for that. So I always plan things you can either make or assemble ahead, and that often leads to a casserole. This one spikes the French toast with bourbon, and blueberries provide sweet bursts throughout the dish. While I'm usually tempted to go for a more traditional buttery brioche or challah bread, for this recipe, I prefer a sturdier artisan loaf, like sourdough. It softens while soaking up the custard yet maintains some structural integrity after it bakes, staying crispy on top, even after you drown it in maple syrup.

1. To a greased 9 x 13-inch (22 x 33cm) baking dish, add the bread pieces and blueberries.
2. To a large bowl, add the eggs, half-and-half, ½ cup of the sugar, the bourbon, butter, 1 teaspoon of the cinnamon, and a pinch of salt. Whisk to thoroughly combine. Pour the egg mixture over the bread and press down to allow the bread to start soaking up the custard.
3. In a small bowl, stir together the remaining tablespoon sugar and ¼ teaspoon cinnamon and sprinkle over the casserole. Cover with aluminum foil and let sit in the refrigerator for at least one hour or overnight.
4. Preheat the oven to 375°F (190°C).
5. Bake covered for 30 minutes, then remove the foil and continue baking for 20 to 25 more minutes, until the top of the casserole is crispy. Serve dusted with the powdered sugar and drizzled with the maple syrup.

use it up!

If you have leftover blueberries, use them in my Mixed-Berry Cardamom Cobbler (page 230).

equipment intel

The best way to get a beautiful even coating of powdered sugar is to put it in a fine-mesh strainer (which you likely have on hand to drain pasta), then gently tap it so it falls like snow right on top of the casserole.

sausage muffin bah-duh-buh-buh-buh-reakfast strata

In the realm of fast-food breakfast, the Sausage McMuffin reigns supreme—far superior to the standard Egg McMuffin, because if Canadian bacon has no haters, then I am dead. Here I've made a strata-fied version to feed a crowd, with English muffins that toast up in the oven and soak up all the flavors of the savory-sweet breakfast sausage bits. You could totally assemble this the night before and toss it in the oven when you wake up, but if you want the muffins to stay a little crispier like I do, I recommend letting the casserole mixture marinate for 5 to 10 minutes. Either way, everyone will be lovin' it.

prep time
25 minutes

cook time
1 hour

yield
serves 6

4 English muffins, cut into bite-size cubes
6oz (170g) hash-brown patties cut into bite-size pieces or frozen tater tots
8oz (225g) breakfast sausage, torn into small pieces
10 large eggs
1 cup whole milk or half-and-half
2 tbsp salted butter, melted
2 tbsp minced chives, plus more to serve
2 tsp garlic powder
½ tsp kosher salt
1½ cups shredded mild cheddar cheese

1. Preheat the oven to 375°F (190°C). Grease a 9 x 13-inch (22 x 33cm) baking dish.
2. To the greased baking dish, add the cubed English muffins and hash-brown patties. Arrange the torn sausage pieces around and on top of the muffins and hash browns.
3. Transfer to the oven and cook for 10 minutes, until the bread is toasty and the sausage is cooked. Let sit on the counter for 15 minutes to cool.
4. Meanwhile, in a large bowl, whisk together the eggs, milk, butter, chives, garlic powder, and salt until thoroughly combined. Pour into the dish and press the bread gently to submerge, then sprinkle in the cheese.
5. Cover with foil and bake for 30 minutes, then remove the foil and bake for another 15 minutes, until the eggs are set. Serve topped with more chives.

don't mess it up!

If you add the egg mixture while the casserole dish is still hot, straight out of the oven, it will immediately start to set the eggs around the edges, which will lead to uneven cooking. So don't skip the cooling of the pan if you want it to come out perfect!

use it up!

If you have leftover chives, they are easy to use up in my Green Godd-ish salad dressing (page 73) or in my Sweet Potato & Asparagus Fri-tot-a (page 47)!

smoked salmon & avocado croissants
honey-dijon praline bacon

sweet potato &
asparagus
fri-tot-a

30ish minutes

one dish

smoked salmon & avocado croissants

with lemon-pepper cream cheese

prep time
20 minutes

cook time
5 minutes

yield
makes 12 croissants

12 mini croissants
8oz (227g) container whipped cream cheese
Zest and juice of 1 lemon
2 tsp freshly ground black pepper, plus more to serve
1 tsp kosher salt, divided
8oz (225g) smoked salmon
2 avocados, sliced
2oz (60g) fresh arugula
1 tbsp olive oil
¼ cup drained capers (optional), to serve

Lemon with black pepper is one of my favorite flavor combinations, but I've got a strong aversion to almost all store-bought lemon-pepper seasonings, which often have an acrid, metallic taste. The good news is that you can simply mix grated lemon zest with freshly ground black pepper for a much more vibrant alternative that is perfect for spicing up chicken wings or finishing a creamy pasta sauce. Here, you'll stir it into whipped cream cheese, which complements the arugula's natural pepperiness while brightening up the smoked salmon. Of course, you could pile this all on toasted bagels, but I think mini croissants are an unexpected twist that look totally chic on a brunch table.

1. Preheat the oven to 325°F (160°C).
2. On a sheet tray, arrange the croissants and transfer to the oven. Bake for 5 minutes, until warmed through.
3. Directly into the cream-cheese container, add the lemon zest, black pepper, and ½ teaspoon of the salt, and stir to combine.
4. To a medium bowl, add the avocado and arugula and toss with the olive oil, lemon juice, and the remaining ½ teaspoon salt.
5. Arrange the croissants on a platter. Layer each with a generous schmear of the cream cheese, followed by the salmon and the avocado and arugula salad. Finish with more freshly cracked black pepper and the drained capers, if using.

30ish minutes

6 ingredients

one dish

honey-dijon praline bacon

prep time
10 minutes

cook time
25 minutes

yield
serves 6

12 slices of thick-cut bacon
1 tbsp honey
2 tsp Dijon mustard
1 tsp apple cider vinegar
½ cup light or dark brown sugar
½ cup finely chopped pecans

A foolproof method for big-batch bacon is to bake everything in an even layer on a wire rack over a sheet pan, so the fat drips off, leaving you with evenly cooked, crispy strips. This recipe takes me down memory lane to Elizabeth's, a brunch spot in New Orleans known for their iconic praline bacon. It was one of the first times I understood how combining ultra-sweet and ultra-savory ingredients can harmonize rather than clash. The only thing missing was a touch of zip to cut through the richness, so I like to add a vinegar-spiked honey Dijon to meld the elements together. I find these get crispier and tastier as they cool, so serve at room temperature.

sweet potato & asparagus fri-tot-a

30ish minutes

6 ingredients

one dish

There's one piece of kitchen equipment that's essential for never messing up a frittata: a good nonstick, oven-safe skillet. These days, there are multiple great brands that make them (I'm partial to Caraway), or you can use a cast-iron as long as it's well seasoned. It's a choose-your-own-adventure situation with ingredients. I like to go with one part cheese, one part veg, and two parts starch—in this case, sweet-potato tots. I didn't just choose them for a pun in the recipe title; the crispy edges are the ideal textural contrast to the fluffy eggs.

prep time
10 minutes

cook time
25 minutes

yield
serves 4–6

8 eggs
¼ cup whole milk or half-and-half
1 tsp kosher salt
½ tsp freshly ground black pepper
3 tbsp neutral oil, divided
8oz (225g) frozen sweet-potato tots
½ cup asparagus pieces, about 1in (2.5cm) long
4oz (115g) crumbled feta or goat cheese, divided
3 tbsp minced chives, divided

1. Preheat the oven to 375°F (190°C).
2. In a large bowl, mix the eggs with the milk, salt, and black pepper until thoroughly combined and bubbles start to form. Set aside.
3. To a large, oven-safe nonstick or cast-iron skillet over medium-high heat, add 2 tablespoons of the oil and heat until shimmering. Add the frozen tots and cook for 5 minutes, then add the asparagus and cook for 3 minutes, stirring frequently, until the tots start to get crispy all over.
4. Reduce the heat to medium-low and add the remaining tablespoon oil to the pan. Give the eggs another vigorous stir, then pour into the pan and sprinkle in half the cheese and half the chives. Cook for 3 minutes, gently stirring only once or twice, until the eggs start to set around the edges.
5. Transfer to the oven to finish cooking for 12 to 14 minutes, until the eggs are fully set. Top with the remaining cheese and chives, then carefully slide out of the pan, cut into wedges, and serve.

1. Preheat the oven to 375°F (190°C).
2. Place a wire rack on top of a large sheet pan covered with aluminum foil. Lay the bacon slices in an even layer on the rack, transfer to the oven, and bake for 12 minutes, until halfway cooked; they will shrink slightly and start to crisp around the edges.
3. In a small bowl, stir together the honey, Dijon mustard, and apple cider vinegar. In another bowl, mix together the brown sugar and pecans. Brush the bacon with the honey mustard and top with the brown-sugar pecans.
4. Return to the oven and bake for another 10 to 12 minutes, until deep golden brown. Let cool on the rack for at least 10 minutes before serving.

don't mess it up!

Because of all the sugar in the topping, this bacon can burn in the oven pretty quickly if you're not keeping an eye on it. Check periodically to make sure it hasn't gone too far. It should be dark brown but not verging on black, and if it's not super crispy yet, don't worry, as it will crisp up as it cools on the rack.

30ish minutes · 6 ingredients · no chop · one dish

spicy maple chicken-and-waffle sliders

Many days, when I go grocery shopping for recipe development, I show up without a plan. I stroll the aisles, listen to a reality-TV-recap podcast, and diligently study each shelf, waiting for a sign. In this instance, my spirit was moved by the mini Eggo waffles—a frozen snack I didn't know still existed. My mom used to serve them to me slathered in peanut butter every morning before school. In the store, they were located right next to the frozen chicken nuggets (the generic Publix brand is fantastic, in case you were wondering), and it doesn't take a genius to put two and two together. These guys are now internet famous with over ten million views on my social channels, so I had to immortalize them in print. Beyond breakfast, they're also great as a game-day party snack!

prep time
10 minutes

cook time
25 minutes

yield
makes 12 sliders

- 12 frozen chicken nuggets
- 5 tbsp salted butter, melted
- 3 tbsp maple syrup, plus more to serve
- 2 tbsp hot sauce
- 1 tsp Cajun seasoning
- 24 mini frozen waffles

1. Preheat the oven to 375°F (190°C).
2. To each cup of a muffin tin, add one chicken nugget and bake for 10 to 12 minutes, until crispy.
3. To a medium bowl, add the butter, maple syrup, hot sauce, and Cajun seasoning. Toss the chicken in the sauce while hot and set aside.
4. In each cup of the muffin tin, place one mini waffle and bake for 5 minutes, until slightly toasted. Top with the chicken, then another mini waffle, and secure with a toothpick.
5. Brush the tops with excess sauce from the bottom of the bowl and bake for 5 to 7 minutes, until golden. Remove from the pan and serve drizzled with more maple syrup.

ingredient intel

You can use any mini frozen waffle brand you want so long as it fits in your muffin tin—for this photo, we used the Evergreen brand of banana waffles, which are very hearty and add an extra sweetness. But plain mini Eggo waffles work just as great (and are more nostalgic for me, honestly).

6 ingredients

one dish

muffin-tin honey-butter ham and cheese biscuits

prep time
20 minutes

cook time
20 minutes

yield
makes 12 biscuits

If you've never made biscuit dough from scratch, don't stress. Cut your teeth on this three-ingredient, ultra-easy beginner's recipe. Not literally, though; these biscuits are so tender and flaky, your teeth will stay gorgeous. The secret is something I always have on hand: self-rising flour, which already contains baking powder and salt. I like to make this ham and cheese version for Easter brunch, but you may end up wanting them any day of the year.

- 2½ cups self-rising flour
- 6 tbsp chilled salted butter, divided
- 1⅓ cups cold buttermilk, divided
- 8 slices of deli ham, torn into pieces
- 6 slices of Swiss cheese, torn into pieces
- 1 tbsp Dijon mustard
- 1 tbsp honey

1. Preheat the oven to 375°F (190°C). Grease a 12-cup muffin tin with butter or cooking spray.
2. To a large bowl, add the flour. Cut 4 tablespoons of the butter into small cubes and use your hands to gently press them into the flour until the butter breaks down into small, pea-size chunks.
3. Pour in 1 cup of the buttermilk and use a fork to gently incorporate until a shaggy dough forms. If the mixture feels too dry and crumbly, add the remaining buttermilk one splash at a time (see note below).
4. To each cup of the muffin tin, add 1 tablespoon of the dough and spread into a thin, even layer (don't worry, they'll rise). Top each scoop of dough with the ham, cheese, and a thin layer of Dijon mustard. Roll the remaining dough into 12 golf ball-size rounds. Flatten and place on top.
5. Melt the remaining 2 tablespoons of butter and stir together with the honey. Brush the tops of the biscuits with the honey butter.
6. Bake for 12 to 14 minutes, until golden brown. Brush with any extra honey butter and let sit in the muffin tin for 5 minutes before carefully removing with a butter knife or small offset spatula. Serve hot or at room temperature.

don't mess it up!

Biscuit dough can go from too dry and crumbly to wet and sticky really quickly, and it's also at the mercy of the humidity and altitude of your environment, which is why giving exact measurements can be tricky. I like to start with a more modest amount of liquid and add a little more at a time if needed. Even if the dough seems dry, see if you can press it into a small disc without it crumbling apart . . . If so, it's ready.

use it up!

For another way to use self-rising flour and buttermilk, try my Mixed-Berry Cardamom Cobbler (page 230), where it gives a wonderfully fluffy, almost cake-like texture to the batter.

Southernmost Bees
Florida Keys
Raw Honey

6 ingredients

one dish

dollywood-style cinnamon bread

Those of us in the theme-park community know there is no more iconic pre-coaster treat than the Dollywood cinnamon bread, which wafts the sumptuous scent of sugar, warm spices, and yeast through the crisp Smoky Mountains air. Over the years, I've tested countless variations at home using homemade bread dough, but nothing has turned out better than using thawed premade loaves from the freezer aisle. My go-to is Bridgford Ready-Dough, because it has a wonderfully airy texture. Let them rise in the pan coated in a borderline egregious amount of cinnamon-sugar butter, which makes each piece sticky-sweet and caramelized on the outside but soft on the inside, just like Kenny Rogers when he met Dolly. (That will only make sense if you know the lyrics to "Islands in the Stream.")

prep time
20 minutes, plus rising time

cook time
45 minutes

yield
serves 8

- ¾ cup (1½ sticks) salted butter, melted
- ⅔ cup light or dark brown sugar
- 1 tbsp cinnamon
- 1½ tsp vanilla extract, divided
- 3lb (1361g) package frozen bread dough, thawed and each loaf sliced into 8 even pieces
- 2 cups powdered sugar
- ½ tsp kosher salt

1. In a large bowl, whisk together the butter, brown sugar, cinnamon, and 1 teaspoon of the vanilla.
2. Dip each piece of dough into the cinnamon-sugar butter. In a 9½ x 9½-inch (24 x 24cm) baking dish, arrange them in three rows. Cover with a clean kitchen towel and let rise on the counter for two hours, or overnight in the refrigerator. It should double in size. (You should have some leftover cinnamon-sugar butter to brush on after baking.)
3. Preheat the oven to 350°F (180°C). Line a large sheet pan with aluminum foil.
4. Place the pan with the dough on top of the lined baking sheet. Bake for 40 to 45 minutes, until golden brown and a toothpick inserted in the center comes out clean. Remove from the oven and brush with the remaining butter mixture. Let cool slightly in the pan while you make the icing.
5. In a medium bowl, whisk together the powdered sugar, 2 tablespoons water, the remaining ½ teaspoon vanilla extract, and the salt. If the icing looks dry, add a splash more water. Drizzle the icing over the bread before serving.

swap it out

If you can't find the frozen bread dough, you can use frozen (unbaked) yeast dinner rolls, such as the Rhodes brand. Simply thaw them, then follow the directions starting at step 3, nestling as many into the baking dish as can comfortably fit.

30ish minutes

homecomin' shrimp & white cheddar grits

prep time
5 minutes

cook time
30 minutes

yield
serves 6

As one of the nation's foremost Disney World food scholars, I have eaten at all two-hundred-plus dining locations on the property. If I had to choose a favorite based solely on food quality—without taking into account theatrics, flair, or Chip 'n Dale interactions—it would be Chef Art Smith's Homecomin' at Disney Springs. He's a legend in southern-style cooking for revolutionary dishes like his Fried Chicken & Doughnuts. Chef Smith graciously shared with me his recipe for spiced-up shrimp and grits with a kicky tomato sauce. He uses stone-ground grits, which take close to an hour to get tender. I've adapted the recipe with time-saving ingredients for a brunch that comes together super quickly.

1lb (450g) medium shrimp, peeled and deveined
2 tsp Cajun seasoning, divided, plus more to taste
1 cup quick-cooking grits
3 tbsp salted butter
8oz (227g) block white cheddar cheese, grated
Fine kosher salt, to taste
6oz (170g) andouille sausage, diced
1 red, yellow, or orange bell pepper, diced
1 bunch of scallions, sliced
1 cup arrabbiata sauce, such as Rao's

1. In a medium bowl, season the shrimp with 1 teaspoon of the Cajun seasoning and set aside.
2. To a small saucepan over medium-high heat, add the grits and 4 cups water. Bring to a boil, then reduce the heat to medium-low and cook for 7 minutes, until tender. Add the remaining teaspoon Cajun seasoning, the butter, and the cheese, and stir until melted. Season with salt or more Cajun seasoning to taste. Reduce the heat to very low to keep warm while you cook the shrimp, stirring occasionally to prevent the bottom from burning.
3. To a large skillet over medium-high heat, add the sausage and cook for 5 minutes, until crispy and the fat is rendered.
4. Reduce the heat to medium-low and add the bell pepper and scallions to the pan, reserving some of the greens of the scallions to garnish. Cook for another 3 minutes, until slightly softened, then add the shrimp and cook for about 2 minutes per side. Stir in the arrabbiata sauce and cook for 2 more minutes, until bubbling and the shrimp are cooked through.
5. Serve the shrimp and sauce over the grits, and garnish with the remaining scallion greens.

use it up!

If you have leftover arrabbiata sauce, use it for dipping the Garlic-Knot Pigs in a Blanket (page 209) or in place of the marinara sauce in my Eggplant Parm French Bread Pizza (page 123).

don't mess it up!

If the grits seize up a bit while you're cooking the shrimp, just add a couple tablespoons of water (or whole milk), increase the heat to medium, and let them take in the extra liquid. They'll be creamy again and ready to serve.

cheddar biscuits

At Homecomin' they serve their shrimp and grits with homemade cheesy drop biscuits, so if you want to make this even heartier you can serve some on the side. (I just cheat and use the Red Lobster Cheddar Bay Biscuit Mix . . . but don't tell anyone that.)

soups & salads

Come And
Get it

beer cheese broccoli orzo soup

Beer cheese soup—a glorious Midwestern classic—is a food I love that also makes me laugh, because it's kind of amazing to eat a huge bowl of cheesy beer as a meal. This recipe is a hybrid of beer cheese soup and broccoli-cheddar soup, because in my mind, the broccoli gives it more social graces. Add some orzo in there, and you've got a totally comforting and stick-to-your-ribs meal. You can really use any beer you like in this recipe, but I'm partial to a dark beer like Shiner Bock (that's the Texan in me), which lends a deeper, slightly nutty flavor. For something subtler, go with a Miller Lite (that's the Wisconsin in my husband.)

prep time
15 minutes

cook time
25 minutes

yield
serves 6

3 tbsp salted butter
2 small heads of broccoli, finely chopped (by hand or in a food processor)
1 bunch of scallions, sliced
⅓ cup flour
1 tbsp Cajun seasoning or seasoned salt
1 tbsp garlic powder
12oz (354ml) can or bottle of dark beer, such as Shiner Bock
4 cups (1 qt) chicken broth
1 cup orzo
Two 12oz (354ml) cans evaporated milk
1lb (450g) block of sharp cheddar cheese, shredded, plus more to serve
Kosher salt and freshly ground black pepper, to taste

1. In a large pot over medium heat, melt the butter and add the broccoli and most of the scallions, reserving some of the green parts for garnish. Cover with a lid and cook, stirring occasionally, for 3 minutes.
2. Add the flour, Cajun seasoning, and garlic powder and cook for another 2 minutes, stirring constantly. Slowly pour in the beer, stirring constantly, and increase the heat to medium-high. Bring to a simmer and let cook for 3 minutes.
3. Add the chicken broth and orzo, and boil for another 5 to 7 minutes, stirring frequently so the orzo doesn't stick to the bottom.
4. Reduce the heat to low and add the evaporated milk. Simmer until heated through and the orzo is just cooked, about 1 minute.
5. Turn off the heat and slowly stir in the cheese a handful at a time until melted. Season with salt and pepper to taste and serve with the scallion greens as garnish, plus more cheese, if desired (and I do desire).

don't mess it up!

Even though evaporated milk is more stable than cream, it still runs the risk of breaking if boiled at too high a heat. Make sure the soup is at a low simmer when you add it at the end so it doesn't curdle and ruin your whole soup!

why freshly grated cheese?

I know it's tempting to buy a bag of pre-grated cheese, but they generally contain an anti-caking agent that prevents the dish from becoming a smooth soup, so you've really got to grate it yourself.

30ish minutes

6 ingredients

one dish

gochujang chicken & dumplings

prep time
10 minutes

cook time
15 minutes

yield
serves 4

2 tsp neutral oil
1½lb (680g) boneless, skinless chicken breasts, cut into bite-sized pieces
8oz (225g) broccoli florets
Fine kosher salt and freshly ground black pepper, to taste
3 tbsp gochujang
2 cups chicken broth
13½oz (400ml) can coconut milk
12oz (340g) frozen mini wontons

The Texas side of my family would probably have me involuntarily committed if I told them I was making chicken and dumplings any way but traditional. They know it as a classic Southern dish with fluffy dough balls or strips simmered in a rich, hearty broth. The dumplings in this recipe are literal: mini wontons you can snag in the frozen aisle. Gochujang, a slightly spicy, slightly sweet Korean fermented soybean chili paste, packs so much flavor that you don't need any other ingredients in the sauce but a can of coconut milk to balance the heat. So basically this is a completely different dish, but, hey, I thought the play on words was fun.

1. To a large sauté pan over medium heat, add the oil and heat for 2 minutes. Add the chicken and broccoli and season with salt and pepper to taste. Cook for 2 minutes, then reduce the heat to medium-low and cover with a lid for 3 minutes so the broccoli can steam.
2. Remove the lid and push the chicken and broccoli to one side of the skillet; add the gochujang and toast for 1 minute.
3. Deglaze (see note below) with the chicken broth, then shake the can of coconut milk and add it to the pan. Stir and bring to a simmer.
4. Add the frozen wontons and stir frequently for 5 minutes, until they are cooked through.

what is deglazing?

When you're cooking on pretty much any pan, you will usually see some dark bits start to build up on the bottom. Don't be spooked! That is flavor caramelizing on the pan (in this case, the natural fermented sweetness of the gochujang), and when you hit it with a liquid and give it a gentle scrape with your cooking utensil, it will come right off and give the whole dish more depth.

30ish minutes

6 ingredients

curry tomato soup
with chili-garlic naan croutons

I love a not-really-a-recipe recipe, where I can take something from the grocery store and add a few simple ingredients to amp it up, whether you're cooking for family, company, or treating yourself in a pinch. Adding a powerful spice to store-bought tomato soup, for example, lends instant depth. Toast the curry powder in oil first to amplify the flavor (a great tip for any spice, by the way), offering a warmth that balances the sweetness of the tomatoes. The chili-garlic naan croutons are the real game changer. Stirring these crunchy morsels into the steaming hot soup will activate the garlic, perfuming the whole house and instantly transforming the soup.

prep time
10 minutes

cook time
15 minutes

yield
serves 4

4 tbsp olive oil, divided
2 tbsp curry powder
Two 32fl oz (946ml) boxes tomato soup
2 naan flatbreads (such as the Stonefire brand), cut into bite-size pieces
3 garlic cloves, grated or minced
1 Fresno pepper, seeds removed, minced
2 tbsp chopped parsley

1. Preheat the oven to 400°F (200°C).
2. To a large pot over medium heat, add 1 tablespoon of the olive oil and the curry powder. Toast for 1 minute, until fragrant. Add the tomato soup. Stir and reduce the heat to low, then let simmer while you make the croutons.
3. On a large sheet pan, toss the naan with another tablespoon olive oil and transfer to the oven. Bake for 10 minutes, until crunchy.
4. In a small bowl, stir the remaining 2 tablespoons olive oil with the garlic, Fresno pepper, and parsley. Toss the croutons with the chili-garlic mixture in the pan while they are hot. Scatter the croutons onto the soup and serve.

use it up!

If you have leftover parsley, use it to make the chimichurri I put on my Honeymoon Choripán (page 89) or in my Green Godd-ish dressing (page 73). Both sauces are great to have on hand to add flavor to grilled meats and fish!

charred corn & potato chowder

prep time
15 minutes

cook time
45 minutes

yield
serves 4–6

5oz (140g) thick-cut bacon, about 5 slices, chopped
4 garlic cloves, grated or minced
1 bunch of scallions, sliced
3 medium red potatoes, scrubbed and diced
5 cups chicken broth
Two 4oz (113g) cans diced green chiles
2 tsp Cajun seasoning, such as Tony's
12oz (354ml) can evaporated milk
⅔ cup instant mashed potato flakes
12oz (340g) bag frozen fire-roasted corn

Probably the most awesome cooking "hack" I've ever learned on TikTok is that instant mashed potatoes can be used to thicken a soup. You don't have to mess with making a roux; you just toss the flakes in at the end and the rest happens, well, instantly. There's no better time to use that trick than in this soup, because it reinforces the fresh potato flavor that's already in there. Cajun seasoning adds a bold spiciness I prefer, but you can use a standard seasoned salt, which has similar spices but less heat.

1. To a large pot over medium heat, add the bacon and cook for 8 minutes, until crispy and the fat is rendered. Transfer half the bacon onto a small plate, leaving the other half in the pan.
2. To the same pot, add the garlic and most of the scallions, reserving some of the green parts for garnish. Sauté for 1 minute, then add the potatoes, chicken broth, green chiles, and Cajun seasoning. Increase the heat to high and bring to a boil, then cover with a lid and reduce the heat to medium-low. Let simmer, stirring occasionally, for 30 minutes, or until the potatoes are fork tender.
3. Remove the lid and stir in the evaporated milk, instant mashed potatoes, and fire-roasted corn. Let gently simmer for another 5 minutes to thicken, then serve, garnished with the reserved bacon and scallion greens.

make it heartier and carbier

I am a sucker for a bread-bowl soup (chalk it up to all my after-school Panera runs), so if you want to take this meal up a notch, hollow out the top of small round bread loaves and serve it in those. Just allot time for a nap after.

30ish minutes

no chop

one dish

lemon chicken tortellini soup

prep time
5 minutes

cook time
15 minutes

yield
serves 6

---

6 cups chicken broth
4 cups shredded rotisserie chicken (from 1 rotisserie chicken)
8.8oz (249g) package cheese tortellini
6oz (170g) fresh spinach
1 cup store-bought matchstick carrots, (or one large carrot, peeled and grated)
12oz (354ml) can evaporated milk
⅓ cup instant mashed potatoes
1 tsp garlic powder
Juice of 1 lemon
1 tsp kosher salt, plus more to taste

This is my favorite type of recipe because you put every ingredient into a pot, fire up the stove, and within minutes, ta-da, you've got a meal. It's really a blueprint for so many soups: protein, broth, carbs, and veggies. Once again, instant mashed potatoes work their magic as a thickener, giving more body and a little extra flavor. Don't be scared of the instant mashed potatoes!

To a large pot over high heat, add all the ingredients and bring to a boil. Reduce the heat to medium and let simmer for 5 to 7 minutes, stirring occasionally, until the tortellini is cooked through. Season with more salt to taste.

make it how you like it

I find that soup consistency is a very personal journey—some like a brothier and more fluid soup while others prefer a heartier, thicker soup. I like it somewhere in the middle, but this one is easily customizable: Make it as the recipe states, then add some heft by stirring in more instant mashed potatoes at the end, a tablespoon at a time, until you're satisfied.

30ish minutes

one dish

kale & fennel salad
with italian vinaigrette

I love any grocery-store ingredient you can buy in a flavored oil, because that infusion can be repurposed for marinades, sauces, or salad dressings. In this case, the oil from the marinated mozzarella is loaded with flavors like garlic, red pepper, and fresh herbs. Add just a bit of mayonnaise and red wine vinegar, and you get an instant Italian vinaigrette. This chopped kale number is one of those rare salads that you can make and dress a couple hours ahead of time, because the vinegar will break down the tough fibers in the hearty greens and make for an even more pleasant eating experience.

prep time
25 minutes

yield
serves 4

- 12oz (340g) marinated mozzarella balls, marinating oil reserved
- 2 tbsp mayonnaise
- 2 tbsp red wine vinegar
- Kosher salt, to taste
- 1 tsp freshly ground black pepper
- 4oz (115g) kale, chopped
- 1 small head of radicchio, chopped
- 1 small head of fennel, thinly sliced, fronds reserved
- 1 small bunch radishes, sliced
- 2oz (60g) salami, torn into pieces
- ⅓ cup chopped pistachios

1. In a measuring cup, whisk together ½ cup of the mozzarella marinating oil with the mayonnaise and red wine vinegar. Season with the salt and pepper.
2. To a large bowl, add the kale and radicchio. Toss with half the vinaigrette and let sit for at least 10 minutes to soften the greens, or up to 2 hours in the refrigerator (it will get softer the longer it sits).
3. When you're ready to serve, add the fennel, radishes, salami, pistachios, and mozzarella balls and toss with the remaining vinaigrette. Garnish with the fennel fronds.

ingredient intel

Thinly sliced fennel is one of my favorite salad additions because it adds a fresh crunch, it's great for digestion, and the fronds on top make for a beautiful garnish. But eaten raw, it does have a strong anise flavor reminiscent of black licorice, so if you're not into that, I might leave it out or swap in a thinly sliced red onion for a similar crunch.

use it up!

If you have leftover pistachios, use them in my Whipped Ricotta Dip with Pistachio-Artichoke Pesto (page 206). If you're not going to use them quickly, though, store them (and all other nuts) in the freezer. Nuts have oils in them that can make them go rancid quickly at room temperature, and the freezer will extend the shelf life by about 6 months.

30ish minutes

tex-mex chopped salad
with avocado-jalapeño ranch

prep time
20 minutes

cook time
12 minutes

yield
serves 4

This is an at-home take on one of my most cherished restaurant salads, the Mexi-Cobb from the Tex-Mex chain Chuy's. (I grew up going to the original location in Austin, not to brag.) Their tangy, garlicky jalapeño-ranch dressing has become the stuff of legend, and it's easy to whip up a version at home in seconds. My recipe gets its added silkiness, body, and flavor by blending an avocado straight into the dressing.

- 2 tsp neutral oil
- 1½lb (680g) boneless skinless chicken breasts
- 4 tsp fajita or taco-seasoning blend, divided
- ¾ cup store-bought ranch dressing (such as Ken's)
- 3 tbsp diced pickled jalapeños, plus 2 tbsp of the brine
- 2 avocados, divided
- 2 garlic cloves, peeled
- Juice of 1 lemon
- 3 heads of romaine lettuce, chopped
- 2 cups chopped cherry tomatoes (from 1 pint)
- 1 cup crushed corn chips (such as Fritos) or tortilla chips
- 1 cup shredded Monterey Jack cheese, (optional)

1. To a medium skillet over medium heat, add the oil. Season the chicken with 2 teaspoons of the fajita seasoning, then cook in the skillet for 6 minutes per side. Remove from heat and cover with a lid or aluminum foil while you assemble the rest of the salad.
2. To a blender, add the ranch dressing, jalapeños and brine, one of the avocados, garlic, lemon juice, and the remaining 2 teaspoons seasoning, plus 3 tablespoons water. Blend until smooth. If the dressing is too thick, add another splash of water and pulse to your desired consistency.
3. Dice the chicken into bite-size pieces and dice the remaining avocado. To a large bowl, add the romaine, then top with the diced avocado and chicken, the tomatoes, corn chips, and cheese, if using. Toss with the dressing and serve.

don't mess it up!

I find that most beginning cooks are so terrified to undercook chicken breasts that they almost always end up hammering it until it's dry as a bone. About 6 minutes per side in a skillet is usually perfect for me, but the key is letting it rest in the pan off the heat, covered, so the chicken finishes cooking through and traps the moisture inside. The great thing about this recipe is that you'll be able to tell if it's undercooked when you cut into it, so err on cooking it for less time—you can always dice it and throw it back into the skillet for a minute or two until there's no more pink.

buying tomatoes

This is a recipe that could really fall flat with subpar tomatoes. Here, I love heirloom tomatoes in a variety of colors, shapes, and sizes for visual appeal—you can find these at more and more grocery stores nowadays, but if you have a local farmer's market, even better. I used to think the firmest tomatoes were the best to buy, but perfectly ripe tomatoes should actually have just a little bit of give when you press on them gently and shouldn't be mushy. If you're out of season or limited in options, I find that cherry and grape tomatoes have the best year-round quality!

30ish minutes

6 ingredients

crunchy heirloom tomato & goat cheese salad

with green godd-ish dressing

One thing that really cheeses me off is buying big bundles of herbs that end up rotting in the refrigerator because I used only 1 tablespoon in one recipe. Now I grow my own herbs (to varying degrees of success), but if you've been afflicted by this issue, too, then this salad dressing is the remedy. Inspired by a classic Green Goddess dressing—which typically has a mix of fresh herbs blended with garlic, anchovy, olive oil, and something creamy like mayonnaise or yogurt—this version uses goat cheese as the base for a sharp tang that balances the sweet tomatoes. I leave out the anchovy to keep it fully vegetarian, but you could always add in a fillet for a little umami.

Use pretty much any herbs you have on hand, so long as they are tender herbs like fresh parsley, basil, mint, dill, cilantro, chives, or tarragon (which has a slight licorice flavor, so be careful with that if you're not so into that flavor). Heartier herbs like sage, thyme, and rosemary should be avoided as they have a stronger flavor and a harsher texture that's better for cooked dishes.

I finish the salad with crunchy, buttery breadcrumbs because I love a crispy fried goat-cheese salad, and this evokes the same flavor and texture without having to mess around with frying.

prep time
15 minutes

cook time
5 minutes

yield
serves 4–6

- 8oz (225g) goat cheese, crumbled and divided
- 2 cups loosely packed mixed fresh soft herbs, such as parsley, basil, tarragon, or chives
- ⅓ cup extra-virgin olive oil
- 1 tbsp white wine vinegar or champagne vinegar
- 1 garlic clove, peeled
- Kosher salt and freshly ground black pepper, to taste
- 3 tbsp salted butter
- 2 cups panko breadcrumbs
- 2lb (900g) heirloom tomatoes of various sizes, roughly chopped

1. To a food processor, add half of the goat cheese along with the herbs, olive oil, vinegar, garlic, and 2 tablespoons water. Pulse until smooth and season with salt and pepper to taste; set aside.
2. In a medium skillet over medium heat, melt the butter and add the breadcrumbs, stirring constantly for 3 minutes, until a deep golden brown. Season with salt and pepper to taste and remove from the heat to let cool slightly.
3. On a large platter, arrange the tomatoes in an even layer. Drizzle with the dressing and sprinkle with the remaining goat cheese crumbles. Top with the toasted breadcrumbs and serve.

storing tomatoes

There's an old wives' tale that you should never refrigerate tomatoes because it diminishes quality and makes them mealy. I've lost a lot of good tomatoes listening to this advice, leaving them to decay on the counter in just a couple of days. The truth is, almost all grocery store tomatoes have already been refrigerated at some point by the time they've reached your cart, and America's Test Kitchen has even busted this myth, finding that refrigerating tomatoes greatly increases their shelf life with negligible impact on quality. If you find nice ripe tomatoes, though, it's best to eat them immediately—or store them whole in an airtight container in the refrigerator.

slicing tomatoes

To make clean tomato slices, your best friend is a serrated bread knife. The jagged edges will give you beautiful cuts without squishing the tomatoes and losing all the juices to the cutting board.

30ish minutes

one dish

kimchi pasta salad

prep time
15 minutes

cook time
10 minutes

yield
serves 4

Store-bought kimchi is a powerful, ever-present force in my refrigerator. I love to eat it on its own as a snack, chop some up and stir into my scrambled eggs, or throw it on a turkey sandwich to turn a basic lunch into a funky adventure. This pasta-salad dressing has an amped-up flavor from chopped kimchi and some of the juice from the jar, reinforcing the intense flavor and lending an appealing orange hue. I like to use a bag of broccoli slaw, which adds a nutrient-packed crunch.

1lb (450g) cavatappi
1 cup mayonnaise
1 cup chopped kimchi, plus 2 tbsp of the brine
1 tbsp rice vinegar
½ tsp garlic powder
½ tsp ground ginger
12oz (340g) store-bought raw broccoli slaw mix
1 bunch of scallions, sliced
Kosher salt, to taste

1. Add the pasta to a medium pot and cover with water by about 2 inches. Place the pot on the largest burner of your stove over high heat. Add a generous pinch of salt to the water and bring to a boil, stirring occasionally, until the pasta is al dente. Strain and rinse under cold water until cool to the touch.
2. In a large bowl, whisk together the mayo, half of the kimchi plus the brine, the vinegar, garlic powder, and ground ginger. Add the pasta, slaw, and scallions, and toss to coat. Stir in the remaining kimchi and season with salt to taste. Cover and store in the refrigerator until ready to serve.

don't mess it up!

I pretty much never rinse pasta for traditional recipes when it's served hot because you want the starch to help it combine seamlessly with the sauce. For pasta salad, the noodles should always be rinsed to remove that starch. This allows the dressing to coat the pasta without being absorbed too much, and keeps the pasta from sticking together.

make it a meal

As it is, this is more of a side dish for me, but there are so many beautiful additions that can bulk it up. I'll often add shredded rotisserie chicken breast, edamame, sliced bell peppers, and chopped fresh mozzarella—keep it in the fridge, and you have a quick and hearty lunch ready to go.

use it up!

Even though this is the only recipe in the book that calls for kimchi, I find so many unexpected places to sneak it in my diet because it's so delicious and it's very good for your gut health! Dice it up and add it to my Fiery Crab Fried Rice (page 182) or add it to a grilled cheese (page 81) for a funky and exciting crunch.

sandwiches

30ish minutes

6 ingredients

key lime shrimp rolls, two ways

prep time
15 minutes

cook time
10 minutes

yield
makes 6 sandwiches

for the chilled shrimp-roll filling

⅓ cup mayo
Zest and juice of 2 key limes, or 1 regular lime
2 tbsp minced fresh chives or parsley
1½ tsp Old Bay or Cajun seasoning, plus more to taste
1½lb (680g) chilled cooked shrimp, cut into bite-size pieces
Kosher salt, to taste

for the warm shrimp-roll filling

4 tbsp salted butter
3 garlic cloves, grated or minced
1½lb (680g) raw shrimp, peeled, deveined, and cut into bite-size pieces
1½ tsp Old Bay or Cajun seasoning, plus more to taste
2 tbsp minced fresh chives or parsley
Zest and juice of 2 key limes, or 1 regular lime
Kosher salt, to taste

for the buns

6 split-top hot dog buns
5 tbsp salted butter, melted

The first time I visited Key West before I moved here, I went to a spot on Duval Street called The Lobster Shack right around the corner from the famous Southernmost Point Buoy. They have a key lime lobster roll on the menu, which initially weirded me out because I only knew key limes in the context of pie. (I was also a couple of margaritas deep and really dumb about food back then.) Turns out, key limes are just like regular limes, but with a more concentrated tartness that packs a little more of a punch—and especially great for brightening up tender, sweet seafood. For these rolls, I go with shrimp over lobster. It's not only more economical, but the milder flavor and delicate texture make it a blank canvas for soaking in all these flavors.

Now, in terms of preparation, we are a nation divided: Some prefer a warm filling drenched in butter, others a chilled style with mayo. While I'll always go for warm and buttery, when I polled my Instagram followers about which one they wanted in the book, it was a literal fifty-fifty tie. So I gotta give the people what they want: a recipe for each one! You can choose your own adventure, or make both. Even with the chilled mayo filling, though, I still require a toasted buttery roll.

to make the chilled rolls

In a medium bowl, stir together the mayo, key lime zest and juice, chives, and Old Bay. Add the shrimp and gently stir to coat. Season with salt or more Old Bay to taste.

to make the warm rolls

Place a medium skillet over medium heat and melt the butter. Add the garlic, shrimp, and Old Bay, and stir for 2 to 3 minutes, until the shrimp turn pink and are just cooked through. Stir in the chives and key lime zest and juice. Season with salt or more Old Bay to taste.

to assemble the sandwiches

1. Preheat the oven to 375°F (190°C).
2. Place the buns on a sheet tray and brush with the butter. Bake for 5 minutes, until just lightly toasted.
3. Pile the shrimp mixture of your choice into the rolls and serve.

don't mess it up!

Sinking your teeth into rubbery, stringy, overcooked shrimp is one of the more upsetting eating experiences that exists. If you're buying them pre-cooked (like for the chilled rolls), look for shrimp that have a looser C shape rather than a super tight curl, which is an indicator that they are overcooked. When you're cooking them yourself for the warm shrimp rolls, you really just want those small pieces to kiss the pan for a couple of minutes—when they've changed color all over, they are done.

use it up!

If you have leftover key limes, use them in my Key Lime Tiramisu (page 237), which calls for a lot of key lime juice.

Don't mess with Texas

30ish minutes
6 ingredients
no chop
one dish

texas toast grilled cheezies

The grilled cheese is widely considered one of the most basic things to cook, but I'd argue that it's actually more complex than people think. Getting a perfectly golden crust with a molten cheese center requires deft use of the stovetop and the ability to adjust heat on the fly, using a skilled cook's instincts. This hands-off, sheet-pan method fixes those issues and makes a batch of crispy, melty sandwiches that all come out hot at the same time. Try serving it with Curry Tomato Soup (page 63) for a quick and cozy meal.

prep time
5 minutes

cook time
15 minutes

yield
makes 4 sandwiches

⅓ cup mayonnaise
⅓ cup grated Parmesan cheese
2 tsp garlic powder
1 tbsp extra-virgin olive oil
2 tbsp chopped parsley (optional)
8 slices of provolone cheese
8 slices of thick-cut white bread

1. Preheat the oven to 450°F (230°C) and place a sheet pan in the oven while it preheats, about 10 minutes.
2. In a small bowl, stir together the mayonnaise, Parmesan, garlic powder, olive oil, and parsley, if using. Place two slices of cheese between two slices of bread, and brush the outsides of each slice with the Parmesan mayo.
3. Remove the hot sheet pan from the oven and place the sandwiches on it. Transfer to the oven and bake for 12 to 14 minutes, flipping halfway through. When the bread is toasted and the cheese is melted, remove from the oven and serve immediately.

what's the deal with mayo?

If you are skeptical of the mayo on the outside (trust me, I get it), you can use softened butter instead, but I tested it side-by-side and found the mayo yields a more evenly toasty exterior. Even if you're a mayo hater, I promise you won't even know it's there!

30ish minutes

one dish

spicy chicken caesar naan wraps

prep time
15 minutes

cook time
20 minutes

yield
makes 6 wraps

for the dressing

¾ cup mayonnaise
¾ cup grated Parmesan cheese
Zest and juice of 1 lemon
3 tbsp sriracha
2 tbsp extra-virgin olive oil
1 tbsp Worcestershire sauce
½ tsp garlic powder
Kosher salt and freshly ground black pepper, to taste

for the wraps

2 generous handfuls of frozen crinkle fries, about 2 cups
3 cups diced rotisserie chicken
1 large head of romaine lettuce, chopped
½ tsp garlic powder
6 warm mini naan flatbreads, to serve
Grated or shaved Parmesan cheese, to serve

I have taken great joy in seeing chicken Caesar wraps get their time in the social media limelight in recent years, but trends come and go, and I've been a Caesar-wrap evangelist since the days of Myspace. To me, it's the perfect poolside snack. My ideal version follows a couple of rules: First, the chicken should never be hot. We need the lettuce to stay crisp, okay? Second, we have to include french fries—which I like to stuff in the wraps in lieu of croutons. I serve these on store-bought "mini" naan flatbreads, which are usually sold in packs of four (I use the Stonefire brand). They're slightly fluffy and slightly chewy, and since they're about the size of your hand, you can pick them up and eat them like tacos. If you like a more anchovy-forward Caesar dressing, add a teaspoon of anchovy paste, but I like just the minor hint of it you get from the Worcestershire sauce (which typically does have anchovy in it!).

1 To make the dressing, stir together the mayonnaise, Parmesan, lemon zest and juice, sriracha, olive oil, Worcestershire sauce, and garlic powder. Season with salt and pepper to taste.

2 To make the wraps, prepare the frozen fries according to package instructions.

3 To a medium bowl, add the chicken, romaine, and enough of the dressing to lightly coat the salad; reserve the remaining dressing for topping.

4 Season the hot fries with the garlic powder. Pile the salad on each naan and top with the fries, more Caesar dressing, and Parmesan.

simple shortcut

I love to whip up this quick homemade Caesar dressing using ingredients I always have on hand, but you could make this even faster with a store-bought dressing (my favorite is Briannas Asiago Caesar). For this recipe, I'd just add the same amount of sriracha to 1 cup of store-bought dressing . . . and maybe a small squeeze of lemon juice, just to freshen things up.

30ish minutes

one dish

greek salad sandwiches
with whipped red-pepper feta

This five-ingredient whipped red-pepper feta is great on its own as a dip for veggies or pita chips, but I love to use it as a condiment for Greek salad–inspired sandwiches that I pack up and take to the beach (because a beach day without sandwiches is not a proper beach day at all). You can make this a loaded veggie sandwich by leaving out the turkey, but I like the extra protein. Plus, a mild turkey can help tame all the bold flavors from the feta and tapenade. Because this is a saucy sandwich, use the crustiest rolls you can find to soak up the flavor without getting soggy.

prep time
25 minutes

yield
makes 4 sandwiches

- 8oz (225g) feta, preferably packed in brine
- 2 large slices of roasted red bell pepper, roughly chopped
- 1 garlic clove, roughly chopped
- 1 tsp dried oregano, plus more to serve
- 4 tbsp olive oil, plus more to serve
- ⅓ cup kalamata olive tapenade
- 4 crusty sandwich rolls
- 1lb (450g) sliced turkey
- 4 plum tomatoes, sliced
- 1 medium cucumber, sliced
- 1 small red onion, thinly sliced
- Kosher salt, to serve

1. To a food processor, add the feta, roasted red peppers, garlic, oregano, and olive oil. Pulse until smooth.
2. On one side of the sandwich rolls, spread the whipped feta; on the other side, spread the olive tapenade.
3. Assemble the sandwiches with the turkey, tomatoes, cucumber, and onion. Drizzle with the olive oil, a pinch of salt, and more oregano before serving.

ingredient intel

When buying feta for this recipe, I prefer a whole block that's packed in brine (which just means a salty water), because it is creamier, so it will yield a smoother, slicker whipped feta (and you can even blend in a little bit of the brine to loosen up the spread). If you're using dry or pre-crumbled feta, you may need to add a splash of milk to get that creamier consistency.

use it up!

To finish up that jar of roasted red peppers, make my Chopped Italiano Sliders *(page 207).*

30ish minutes

one dish

wasabi avocado chicken salad toasts

prep time
15 minutes

yield
makes 8 toasts

- 4 large, ripe Hass avocados, peeled and pitted
- 1 tbsp wasabi paste
- 1 medium shallot, minced
- Juice of 1 lemon
- 1 tbsp extra-virgin olive oil
- ½ tsp kosher salt, plus more to serve
- 3 cups shredded or diced rotisserie chicken
- 1 small cucumber, chopped
- 8 slices toasted bread, to serve

I was born with an irrational fear of mayonnaise that's taken years of exposure therapy to get over, but one mayo-forward dish I've never been able to get on board with is a classic chicken salad sandwich . . . until I made this version. My take uses smashed avocado and olive oil to provide the creaminess instead! Consider it a cross between avocado toast and a chicken salad sandwich, with a pop of wasabi in there to awaken your senses. I love this on a sturdy toasted sourdough bread, or perhaps even a rye for a deep nuttiness. But truly, use whatever bread you like—that's your own personal journey.

To a large bowl, add the avocados, wasabi paste, shallot, lemon juice, olive oil, and salt; mash together with a fork until well combined. Stir in the chicken and cucumber, and season with salt to taste. Serve on the toast.

make it ahead

You can make a batch of this and keep it in the refrigerator for up to 2 days to whip together an easy snack or lunch, but avocado can quickly oxidize and turn an unappetizing brown color when exposed to air. The lemon juice helps slow this process, so I would add an extra squeeze on top, then store it with plastic wrap directly touching the entire surface to keep it green (same goes for guacamole).

use it up!

Most wasabi paste brands that you buy at the grocery store actually contain a great deal of horseradish, so you can easily swap it in for recipes that call for prepared horseradish, like my Champagne Cocktail Sauce on page 213.

30ish minutes

one dish

honeymoon choripán
with chimichurri

My husband will probably not love it if I publicly state that the best moment of my honeymoon revolved around a sandwich, but listen . . . it's really more of a statement about the power of this sandwich.

When we landed in Buenos Aires after our wedding, we immediately stopped at Nuestra Parrilla, an open-fire barbecue restaurant that's got the best choripán in town. This sandwich is basically chorizo and crusty bread with a zippy chimichurri to cut through the fatty sausage. Across all the fantastic fine-dining meals we had on our trip, our conversation kept coming back to the choripán—so I made an at-home version that saves us a plane ticket. The chimichurri takes five minutes to whip up but only gets better if the flavors marinate over time. Use any extra to enliven grilled steak, chicken, or fish. Oh, and I add provolone cheese, because I love how that sharpness stands up to the chorizo—and because I have impulse-control issues.

prep time
15 minutes

cook time
10 minutes

yield
makes 4 sandwiches

- ¾ cup chopped fresh parsley
- ½ cup chopped cherry or grape tomatoes
- 2 tsp Calabrian chili paste, or ½ tsp red pepper flakes
- 3 garlic cloves, grated or minced
- 1 tbsp red wine vinegar
- 2 tsp extra-virgin olive oil
- Kosher salt, to taste
- 1lb (450g) Argentinean or Mexican chorizo (see note below)
- 4 Italian hoagie rolls (trim the ends if longer than 6 inches)
- 8 slices of provolone cheese

1. Preheat the broiler to low.
2. In a bowl, mix together the parsley, tomatoes, chili paste, garlic, vinegar, olive oil, and a pinch of salt (the chorizo is already salty, so go easy). Stir to combine and set the chimichurri sauce aside.
3. Slice each link of chorizo lengthwise down the middle to open the casing, without cutting all the way through. Pull them open slightly to make a wider patty, keeping the casing on so the shape stays intact. If the chorizo came in bulk rather than links, form into four 6-inch long logs, then flatten slightly. On a foil-lined sheet pan, place the sausages and broil for 5 minutes, until slightly crisped on the edges and cooked through. Remove from the oven, let cool slightly, and remove the casing.
4. Onto each roll, lay 2 slices of the provolone. Place the rolls onto the sheet pan and top each with the chorizo. Return to the broiler for about 2 more minutes, until the cheese is melted and the sausage is fully cooked through. Top with 2 spoonfuls of the chimichurri, close the sandwiches, and serve.

ingredient intel

Argentinian and Mexican chorizo look similar, but the difference is in the spices. Argentinian chorizo has a pronounced paprika and garlic flavor, while the Mexican version has more heat from spicy red chilis. I've found Argentinean chorizo is more common in grocery stores lately, but I've tried this recipe with both types, and it's fantastic either way. Just don't use Spanish chorizo, which is cured and will not give you the right flavor or texture for this dish (but use it for my Spanish Chorizo & Swiss Chard Paella, page 163!).

use it up!

If you have leftover Calabrian chili paste, use it in my Mascarpone Rigatoni alla Vodka (page 102), my Braised Chicken with Italian Beans and Greens (page 142), or my Parmesan Pork Chops with Calabrian Chili Cauliflower (page 152).

30ish minutes

no chop

one dish

bologna sandwiches au cheval

prep time
5 minutes

cook time
15 minutes

yield
makes 4 sandwiches

- ½ cup mayonnaise
- 1½ tbsp Dijon mustard
- 2 tsp apple cider vinegar
- 1 tsp garlic powder, divided
- 2 tbsp salted butter
- 4 brioche burger buns
- 32 thin slices of beef bologna
- 8 slices of sharp yellow cheddar cheese

Au Cheval is a restaurant in Chicago and New York known for their burgers, but what I like even better is their bologna sandwich. It's stacked cartoonishly high with thinly shaved, pan-seared bologna slices layered with melty cheddar cheese, oozing with a garlicky Dijon mayonnaise. This is a slightly more reserved version, with only eight slices of bologna per sandwich instead of, like, a hundred. I like to get the meat from the deli counter and have them shave it as thinly as possible. And if you have any leftover Dijonnaise, use it in salad dressings (just add olive oil and a little extra vinegar) or as a dip for pretzel snacks.

1. In a small bowl, whisk together the mayonnaise, mustard, vinegar, and ½ teaspoon of the garlic powder; set aside.
2. In a large nonstick skillet over medium heat, melt the butter, then place the buns cut-side down for 2 minutes, until toasted. Remove from the pan and sprinkle with the remaining ½ teaspoon garlic powder while the buns are hot.
3. Stack 4 bologna slices into 8 piles. Working in batches of 4 stacks at a time in the same hot skillet, sear the bologna for 3 minutes, until they crisp up on the bottom and around the edges. Flip the bologna and crisp on the other side. (They will shrink as they cook, allowing you to add more stacks to the pan.)
4. Top each with a slice of cheese, cover with a lid, and cook for 2 minutes, until the cheese melts.
5. Place two bologna stacks on the bottom of each burger bun, generously spread Dijonnaise on the top buns, and close the buns. Serve immediately.

ingredient intel

You may notice I use garlic powder in a lot of recipes in lieu of fresh garlic, and there is a reason for that. Garlic powder has a nice, concentrated punch of garlic flavor without the harsh bite of a raw clove of garlic, which makes it great in uncooked preparations. It also disperses evenly in sauces like this Dijonnaise.

pasta & pizza

30ish minutes
6 ingredients
no chop
one dish

burst tomato–basil tortellini
with burrata

prep time
5 minutes

cook time
25 minutes

yield
serves 4

12oz (340g) cherry or grape tomatoes
1 cup white or rosé wine
1½ cups passata
½ tsp red pepper flakes (optional)
20oz (567g) package refrigerated tortellini
¼ cup basil, torn into pieces, plus more to serve
Pinch of kosher salt
4oz (113g) ball of burrata cheese
Extra-virgin olive oil, to serve

After years of consuming food content on social media, I've witnessed some unspeakable acts performed on burrata. The beauty of this ball of cheese lies in the textural contrast between the soft-but-sturdy mozzarella exterior and the creamy stracciatella center. Cooking it totally ruins what makes it special, so instead, we're going to use the burrata as a finishing touch that takes center stage.

1 To a large skillet or sauté pan over medium-high heat, add the tomatoes, wine, passata, and red pepper flakes, if using. Once simmering, reduce the heat to medium-low, cover with a lid, and cook for 15 minutes, stirring occasionally, until the tomatoes are softened.

2 Use the back of a spoon to gently burst the tomatoes, then add the tortellini, basil, and a pinch of salt. Stir to coat; cover with a lid and simmer for 4 to 6 minutes, until the pasta is cooked through, stirring 2 to 3 times as it cooks.

3 Remove from the heat, then break the burrata into pieces and add it to the skillet—it has a soft center and will spill once opened. Garnish with more basil and a drizzle of extra-virgin olive oil before serving.

don't mess it up!

Tortellini is usually pretty delicate and can easily stick to the bottom of the pot, so be sure to stir it a couple of times while it's simmering in the sauce to prevent that. Also, it cooks really fast and tends to get mushy if you take it too far, so check it at exactly 4 minutes to see if it's done, as some brands will cook faster than others.

use it up!

Since burrata is also often served in a package of two, I usually snack on the extra ball with vegetables or crostini—which would be a great addition to a no-cook Italian party spread (pages 204–205)!

30ish minutes

no chop

spicy edamame peanut noodles

Whenever I'm at a Thai restaurant and peanut noodles are on the menu, I'm going to order them. Whenever I'm at a Japanese restaurant, and they have spicy edamame on the menu, I'm going to order them. So why can't we have it all? I've never been a huge PB&J guy, but I love adding a spoonful of peanut butter into a stir fry. Here, it's the hefty backbone of a shortcut peanut sauce (which is also great to serve with grilled chicken skewers for a chicken satay vibe). Plus, the frozen edamame cooks right in the water with the noodles, saving you from dirtying another pot, while getting dinner on the table in about 20 minutes.

prep time
10 minutes

cook time
10 minutes

yield
serves 4

- 2 tbsp neutral oil
- ½ tsp red pepper flakes
- ½ tsp garlic powder
- 2 tbsp sambal oelek
- ⅓ cup Thai sweet chili sauce, plus more to drizzle
- ½ cup creamy peanut butter
- 1 tbsp soy sauce
- Juice of 1 lime
- 12oz (340g) package frozen shelled edamame
- 14oz (400g) wide rice noodles or pad thai noodles
- Crushed peanuts, to serve (optional)
- Cilantro, to serve (optional)

1. Bring a large pot of water to a boil.
2. Meanwhile, in a medium nonstick skillet over medium heat, add the oil. Add the red pepper flakes and garlic powder and cook until sizzling, about 30 seconds. Add the sambal, chili sauce, peanut butter, soy sauce, and lime juice, cook for about a minute until slightly darkened in color, then transfer to a large bowl.
3. Once the pot of water is boiling, add the noodles and edamame and boil for 5 minutes, until cooked through. Add 1 cup of the cooking water to the peanut-butter mixture and whisk to combine and loosen the sauce.
4. Drain the noodles and edamame and rinse under cold water for 30 seconds, then add to the bowl with the peanut sauce and use tongs to stir gently to coat. Transfer to a serving platter (if you want . . . I don't) and carefully drizzle with 1 tablespoon of sweet chili sauce. Top with the crushed peanuts and cilantro leaves, if using.

ingredient intel

Sambal oelek is one of my favorite pantry ingredients, and it brings the heat. It's like an edgier sriracha, with a little more tang, spice, and texture. If you like it, use it in my Hoisin Chicken Lettuce Wraps (page 141) or my Fiery Crab Fried Rice (page 182) in place of the sriracha!

chili crisp noodles
with bok choy

prep time
10 minutes

cook time
15 minutes

yield
serves 4

- 1 tbsp neutral oil
- 1lb (450g) ground pork
- 2 tbsp soy sauce, plus more to drizzle
- 1 bunch of scallions, sliced, green and white parts separated
- 4 garlic cloves, grated or minced
- 3 tbsp spicy chili crisp, such as Lao Gan Ma, plus more to drizzle
- 15.5oz (439g) can chickpeas, with the liquid
- ¾ cup chicken broth
- 2 tbsp rice vinegar
- 8oz (225g) Chinese chow mein stir-fry noodles
- 1lb (450g) bok choy, sliced

The most adventurous trip I've ever taken was to Chongqing, which has been dubbed China's "cyberpunk city" because the skyline turns into a spectacular LED show each night, and the whole place feels like a fever dream. But for me, the most thrilling aspect of the place was the food. Chongqing cuisine is known for the bold and very liberal use of tongue-tingling chili peppers, a striking, almost floral scent that wafts enticingly through the streets. The signature dish is xiǎo miàn, meaning "small noodles," served piping hot with Sichuan chili oil, blanched greens, and a rich pork broth.

An exact recreation requires ingredients I'll simply never find at my island grocery store, but I can get pretty close with readily available items like chili crisp (a spicy pepper–infused oil generally amped up with other flavors like fried garlic and shallots). The traditional version of this dish uses yellow peas for a hearty, slightly crunchy addition, but I've found chickpeas are a great, easy swap here. And as for the noodles, if you can find fresh thin wheat noodles in the refrigerator section of the grocery store, that is most delightful—but the dried kind in the international pantry aisle works great, too.

1. Bring a large pot of salted water to a boil.
2. Meanwhile, in a large skillet over medium-high heat, add the oil and pork. Let brown for 7 to 8 minutes, stirring frequently, then add the soy sauce, scallion whites, and garlic. Cook for another 2 minutes, until the soy sauce is absorbed.
3. Add the chili crisp and cook for 1 minute, then pour in the chickpeas with the liquid, broth, and rice vinegar. Reduce the heat to low and let simmer gently.
4. Once the pot of salted water is boiling, cook the noodles and bok choy for 2 to 3 minutes, until the noodles are tender. Drain and add to the sauce, stirring to coat. Add additional chili crisp for more spice, if desired, and a drizzle of soy sauce for more salt. Serve topped with the scallion greens.

6 ingredients

no chop

20-clove roasted garlic pasta al limone

Oh, here we go again: another recipe inspired by my "days in New York." But listen, there's a restaurant in my old neighborhood called Lil' Frankie's, and their Spaghetti Limone is so incredible, it's one of those dishes I still dream about all the time. I wanted to make a slightly creamier version that's rounded out with a lot of garlic . . . Twenty cloves, because twenty-one seems excessive and nineteen is a weird number. Roasting them until they're sweet and tender results in a silky, tangy, luxurious sauce. I love to use evaporated milk rather than heavy cream because it's shelf stable and lasts a long time, plus it's less likely to break from the acidity of the lemon. Be sure to buy pre-peeled garlic from the grocery store, unless you want to peel twenty cloves by hand.

prep time
15 minutes

cook time
45 minutes

yield
serves 4

- 20 peeled garlic cloves
- 1 tbsp neutral oil
- 12oz (354ml) can evaporated milk
- 5oz (140g) grated pecorino cheese, plus more to serve
- Zest and juice of 1 lemon, plus more juice to taste
- ½ tsp kosher salt, plus more to taste
- ½ tsp freshly ground black pepper, plus more to serve
- 1lb (450g) spaghetti, bucatini, or fettuccine
- 3 tbsp butter

1. Preheat the oven to 350°F (180°C).
2. On a sheet of aluminum foil, place the garlic and coat with the oil. Wrap the foil to fully encase the garlic, then bake for 30 minutes, until a deep golden brown.
3. To a blender, add the roasted garlic, evaporated milk, cheese, lemon zest and juice, salt, and pepper. Blend until very smooth and set aside.
4. Bring a large pot of salted water to a boil and cook the pasta according to package instructions until al dente. Reserve at least 1 cup of the pasta water before draining.
5. Meanwhile, in a separate large skillet over medium-low heat, gently heat the creamy lemon-garlic sauce and melt in the butter. Add the cooked pasta along with half the reserved pasta water and let cook in the sauce for 2 minutes. If you want it saucier, add more pasta water. Taste and add more salt and lemon juice as desired. Serve with the additional cheese and black pepper.

don't mess it up!

The success of this sauce really depends on adding enough pasta water at the end to get the right consistency, so don't forget to save that water before you drain! The best way to do this is to dip a heatproof glass measuring cup directly in the water, or ladle it into the measuring cup if you're more sensitive to the heat from the pot.

simple shortcut

I sang the praises of buying pre-peeled garlic at the beginning of this book, and nowhere is that more necessary than for this recipe. You'll save yourself at least 10 to 15 minutes of peeling garlic—and days of trying to scrub your hands of the scent of garlic.

30ish minutes

mascarpone rigatoni alla vodka

prep time
10 minutes

cook time
20 minutes

yield
serves 4–6

- 1lb (450g) rigatoni or other short pasta
- 2½ tsp kosher salt, divided, plus more to taste
- 4 tbsp salted butter, divided
- 1 medium shallot, sliced
- 2 garlic cloves, minced
- ⅓ cup tomato paste
- 1–2 tbsp Calabrian chili paste
- ⅓ cup vodka
- 1 cup passata
- 8oz (225g) mascarpone cheese
- ⅓ cup grated Parmesan cheese, plus more to serve

One of my favorite shortcuts, born out of laziness but later validated by science, is to start cooking pasta in cold water. I do this only with dried short pasta shapes that can be fully submerged, as longer pastas like spaghetti need boiling-hot water to become pliable enough to fit in the pot, and fresh pastas, like egg pappardelle, cook so fast you need only plop them in boiling water for a minute or two.

Here's why the cold-water method works: The pasta spends more time in the pot releasing starches. That's ideal for any recipe that calls for adding starchy pasta water to a dish, yielding a smooth, cohesive sauce. I swap the usual heavy cream for mascarpone cheese, too, lending an even silkier texture.

I like my vodka pasta extra spicy, so I use 2 whole tablespoons of the Calabrian chilis—but I would go with half, or even a quarter, if you're hesitant. You can always add more later.

1. To a medium pot, add the pasta, enough cold water to cover the pasta by 2 inches, and 2 teaspoons of the salt. Over high heat, bring to a boil, stirring occasionally to prevent the pasta from sticking to the bottom. Once boiling, reduce the heat to medium and cook for 8 minutes, until just shy of al dente (see note below). Reserve 1½ cups pasta water. Drain and set aside.
2. Meanwhile, in a large skillet over medium heat, melt 2 tablespoons of the butter, and add the shallot. Cook for 3 minutes, until slightly softened, then add the garlic, tomato paste, and chili paste. Let toast, stirring constantly, for another 2 minutes, until maroon in color. Pour in the vodka and cook for 2 more minutes, until reduced by half.
3. Reduce the heat to medium-low and add the passata, mascarpone, and the remaining ½ teaspoon salt; stir until the mascarpone melts into the sauce, and let simmer for 5 minutes. Stir in the remaining 2 tablespoons butter and the reserved pasta water.
4. Add the pasta to the sauce and stir in the Parmesan; cook the pasta for another 2 minutes in the sauce until it all comes together and is slick and glossy. Season with salt to taste, and serve topped with more Parmesan.

use it up!

If you have leftover Calabrian chili paste, use it in my Honeymoon Choripán with Chimichurri (page 89), my Braised Chicken with Italian Beans and Greens (page 142), or my Parmesan Pork Chops with Calabrian Chili Cauliflower (page 152).

don't mess it up!

It's surprisingly easy to overcook rigatoni, and you'll notice it because the pasta will start to flatten and tear in spots rather than maintain its tubular shape. That's why it's important to keep an eye on it and drain the pasta while it's still a little underdone, saving a lot of that pasta water so it can finish cooking in the sauce. Keep tasting frequently until it's perfect for your journey, and if you start to see even one piece of pasta tearing, it's time to pull the heat.

30ish minutes

6 ingredients

no chop

brown butter tomato & corn pappardelle

I'm really not one of those cooks who's obsessive about seasonality, and I'm certainly not above buying a supermarket tomato in January if the mood strikes, but this is one recipe I prefer to cook in late August and September when tomatoes and corn are at their peak. Once pumpkin-spice lattes are prematurely back on the menu, making this pasta is like a Pavlovian fight-or-flight response to desperately cling to the last days of summer. The brown butter gives an underlying warm, nutty background that complements the bright, fresh tomato puree and sweet corn, both of which only need to be barely warmed through to maintain their flavor.

prep time
10 minutes

cook time
10 minutes

yield
serves 2–4

1½lb (680g) tomatoes
5 tbsp salted butter
Corn kernels from 1 cob
Kosher salt and freshly ground black pepper, to taste
8oz (225g) pappardelle
Fresh basil, to serve
Shaved Parmesan cheese, to serve

1. Using the largest holes of a box grater placed in a medium bowl, carefully grate the tomatoes to create a chunky tomato puree.
2. To a large skillet over medium heat, add the butter and cook for 3 to 5 minutes, swirling the pan around and stirring frequently, until foaming and brown bits start to form. Add the tomatoes and corn kernels and cook for 2 minutes, until just warmed through. Remove from the heat and season with salt and black pepper to taste.
3. Meanwhile, bring a medium saucepan of water to a boil and add a big pinch of salt. Add the pappardelle and cook according to package directions. Drain, transfer the pappardelle to the sauce, and use tongs to toss the pasta and the sauce together. Garnish with the basil and Parmesan before serving.

don't mess it up!

Brown butter turns to burnt butter in mere seconds, so be cautious. Once it starts to foam so rapidly that you can't see the bottom of the pan, I cut the heat and let the foam settle so I can assess the situation. There should be a layer of dark-brown bits at the bottom of the pan, but not black bits. Let your nose guide you: Brown butter smells rich and nutty, while burnt butter smells acrid and unpleasant.

rosé linguine
with clams

prep time
20 minutes

cook time
20 minutes

yield
serves 4

2lb (900g) littleneck clams
Handful of kosher salt
6 tbsp salted butter, cubed, divided
5 garlic cloves, minced
2 cups rosé wine
16oz (450g) linguine nests, such as Flora
½ cup finely chopped Italian parsley
Juice of 1 lemon
½ tsp red pepper flakes

Ina Garten has always told me never to cook with a wine you wouldn't drink, and I don't really drink white wine. I pretty much always substitute with rosé, which is particularly lovely in linguine with clams because the wine's fruity floral character complements the natural sweetness of the shellfish. A lot of butter tames the tartness of the rosé, providing balance to the whole equation. Make this to impress dinner-party guests or for date night. You'll win points for gorgeous presentation and delicious food, without any stress before dinnertime.

1. In a bowl, cover the clams with cold water and stir in the salt to draw out any sand or grit. Let sit for 15 minutes. Meanwhile, bring a large pot of salted water to a boil.
2. To a large sauté pan over medium-low heat, add 1 tablespoon of the butter and the garlic. Pour in the wine and add the clams. Cover with a lid and cook for 8 to 10 minutes, or until the clams open up. As soon as the clams open up, transfer them to a bowl to stop them from overcooking. Discard any that don't open up and turn the heat down to low.
3. Drop the linguine in the boiling water and cook for about 3 to 4 minutes, until just shy of al dente. Use tongs to transfer the pasta right into the skillet with the sauce, along with two ladles of the pasta water.
4. Stir in the remaining 5 tablespoons butter, the parsley, lemon juice, and as much of the red pepper flakes as you want. Season with salt to taste. Add the clams back in and serve.

buying fresh clams

This can be an intimidating endeavor if you've never done it before. The first time I cooked with them, I was terrified of serving someone a bad clam. But the most important thing is to make sure all the shells are intact (no cracks) and are tightly closed. If a clam shell is even slightly open and doesn't close when you push it back together, don't buy it. The fishmonger should check all of them for you, but it's always good to walk in with this knowledge and make sure they do.

cooking fresh clams

Clams will generally cook at different rates, so you should check them periodically while they are in the skillet and remove them immediately when they open up to avoid overcooking them and to keep them juiciest. Clams that don't open at all (I give it about 12 minutes of cooking) were likely dead before you started cooking them and are therefore dangerous to eat, so that's why we discard them.

30ish minutes

no chop

one dish

chipotle cheddar hamburger helper

I did not grow up in a Hamburger Helper family. That is not to sound elitist; we actually just leaned more on Easy Mac or Rice-A-Roni. I was ever tantalized by that red-and-white box, though, maybe because that hand had a face on it? Now that I'm a grown-up, I can make it on my own (usually when my niece and nephew demand it), with pantry staples, ground beef, cheddar cheese, and spinach (I'm always looking for ways to use up that big bag of greens I buy weekly, and this a good place to sneak them in). The fusilli catches all the bits of sauce in its little curls, and the chipotle puree gives a barely there smokiness that will have everyone coming back for seconds.

prep time
10 minutes

cook time
20 minutes

yield
serves 4

- 1 tbsp neutral oil
- 1lb (450g) ground beef
- 1 tbsp chili powder
- 2 tsp garlic powder
- 1 tsp kosher salt, plus more to taste
- 1lb (450g) short pasta, such as fusilli, shells, or elbows
- 3 cups beef broth
- 12oz (354ml) can evaporated milk
- 8oz (225g) cheddar cheese, shredded
- 2 tbsp chopped chipotles in adobo sauce or chipotle puree
- 5oz (140g) baby spinach
- Juice of 1 lime

1. To a large, 5-quart sauté pan over medium-high heat, add the oil and heat until shimmering. Add the beef, chili powder, garlic powder, and salt. Cook for 8 to 10 minutes, crumbling the meat with the back of a spoon, until browned.
2. Add the pasta, beef broth, and a big pinch of salt. Bring to a boil, then reduce the heat to medium. Cook for 6 minutes, stirring frequently, until the pasta is almost cooked through.
3. Reduce the heat to low and add the evaporated milk, then add the cheese a handful at a time, stirring between each addition, until fully melted into the sauce.
4. Stir in the chipotles, spinach, and lime juice and cook for 2 more minutes, until the spinach is wilted. Remove from the heat, season with more salt to taste, and serve.

ingredient intel

Chipotle peppers in adobo sauce are dried and smoked jalapeños that have been rehydrated in a thick, vinegar-spiked tomato sauce. For this recipe, I like to buy a jar of the La Costeña brand peppers that are already finely chopped, but if you can't find them, simply buy a can of chipotle peppers in adobo sauce and chop them yourself—or better yet, add the whole can to a small food processor and puree it. You can store the excess in the refrigerator and stir it into sauces, marinades, and braises. It's especially good in chili, so try stirring a tablespoon into the filling of my Chicken Chili Tot Pie (page 145) for a touch of smoky spice.

30ish minutes

no chop

one dish

laze-agna

prep time
5 minutes

cook time
25 minutes

yield
serves 4

1 tbsp neutral oil
1lb (450g) hot or mild Italian turkey sausage
2 tsp Italian seasoning
1 tsp garlic powder
24oz (680g) jar marinara or arrabbiata sauce
4 cups chicken broth
1lb (450g) broken lasagna noodles or Mini Lasagne egg noodles, such as Bechtle
3 tbsp pesto, plus more to serve
15oz (425g) ricotta, divided
2 cups shredded mozzarella cheese

There are times when I really want to put in the hours to make a perfectly layered lasagna, alternating a simmered-all-day-long Bolognese sauce and a creamy bechamel. Then there are times when I go full Garfield and need to shove some lasagna in my face immediately. This recipe is for the latter. It has all the appeal of a labor-intensive lasagna, but the ingredients are cooked in one pot. Just pop it under the broiler to melt the cheese at the end, and you've got yourself a weeknight-friendly meal.

1. Preheat the broiler to high.
2. To a large 5-quart, oven-safe sauté pan or pot over medium-high heat, add the oil and sausage and cook for 8 minutes, until the sausage is browned and crumbled. Add the Italian seasoning and garlic powder and cook for 1 more minute, then pour in the marinara sauce, broth, and ½ cup water; bring to a simmer, and reduce the heat to medium.
3. Add the noodles and let simmer for 8 minutes, stirring frequently, until the pasta is almost cooked. Stir in the pesto and half the ricotta and simmer for another 2 minutes. (I like this extra saucy because it will thicken more under the broiler, so if it looks dry, you can add more water.)
4. Top with the mozzarella and scatter the remaining ricotta all over. Broil for 5 minutes, until the cheese is melted. Garnish with dollops of pesto on top.

don't mess it up!

Certain brands of lasagna are thicker and starchier than others, and those will absorb more liquid before they are fully cooked. I like to use the Bechtle "Mini Lasagne" egg noodles because they are thinner and cook faster, but if you're using a thicker noodle, you might need to add more liquid (water, broth, or marinara sauce) so it's the right consistency.

use it up!

If you have leftover pesto, stir a tablespoon or so into my Burst Tomato-Basil Tortellini (page 94) at the end of cooking to reinforce the basil flavor that's already in there.

30ish minutes

6 ingredients

no chop

cheesy butternut squash pasta bake

I have always lived in a canned soup–positive household, and I've carried this ethos into adulthood as the landscape of store-bought soups has greatly improved. Here, a box of butternut squash soup gets bulked up with Italian sausage, fresh thyme and Parmesan, which provides a salty balance to the sweet squash. Consider this a cross between mac and cheese and a more elevated canned-soup noodle casserole than the kind I grew up eating in Texas.

prep time
5 minutes

cook time
30 minutes

yield
serves 4

1lb (450g) pasta shells
1 tsp kosher salt, plus more to taste
1lb (450g) hot or mild Italian sausage, preferably bulk instead of links
2 tbsp fresh thyme leaves, plus more to garnish
32oz (946ml) box butternut squash soup, such as the Pacific Foods brand
1 cup grated Parmesan cheese
8oz (225g) fresh mozzarella cheese, torn into pieces

1. Preheat the broiler to high.
2. To a medium pot, add the pasta, enough cold water to cover the pasta by 2 inches, and 1 teaspoon salt. Bring to a boil over high heat, stirring occasionally to prevent the pasta from sticking to the bottom. Once boiling, reduce the heat to medium and cook for 6 minutes, until a couple minutes shy of al dente (it will finish cooking in the sauce). Drain and set aside.
3. Meanwhile, in a large, oven-safe sauté pan or braiser over medium-high heat, add the sausage and cook for 8 to 10 minutes, crumbling with the back of a spoon, until browned. Add the thyme and butternut squash soup, bring to a simmer, and let it cook down for 10 minutes.
4. Add the pasta and cook in the sauce for 3 minutes, then stir in the Parmesan cheese to thicken the sauce. Season with salt to taste, then top with the mozzarella cheese.
5. Transfer to the oven and broil for about 3 minutes, until browned and bubbly. Let sit for at least 5 minutes to allow the sauce to thicken more, then garnish with additional thyme and serve.

what does "al dente" mean?

It may be common vernacular to those of us who cook a lot (and to Italians, of course), but for those who don't know, "al dente" means "to the tooth" in Italian, referring to pasta that is still firm with just a little bite (and therefore not overcooked). Generally, you want to stop cooking pasta when it's about 1 minute short of al dente so it can finish that final minute of cooking in the sauce. For this recipe, I drain it even earlier to let the pasta finish cooking in the sauce for 3 minutes before getting broiled, which continues the cooking a bit further.

use it up!

If you have leftover thyme, throw the sprigs in my Buttery Roasted Cod (page 178) or add a couple of tablespoons to the tomato sauce in my Baked Brie Ratatouille (page 198).

30ish minutes

6 ingredients

no chop

one dish

one-pot pancetta, kale & mushroom orecchiette

prep time
10 minutes

cook time
25 minutes

yield
serves 4

4oz (115g) diced pancetta
2 tbsp olive oil, divided
5oz (140g) sliced shiitake mushrooms
1lb (450g) orecchiette pasta
4 cups (1 qt) chicken broth
Kosher salt, to taste
1 bunch of Tuscan kale, torn into bite-size pieces (about 2 cups total)
4oz (115g) garlic and herb goat cheese
Freshly ground black pepper, to taste

I spent many years hating on one-pot pastas, and I maintain that I'm mostly on the right side of history. Not all pasta shapes are conducive to this method, but I've since determined that orecchiette is the best for the one-pot route. It cooks quickly and doesn't get gloopy or soggy in the way I've found longer pastas do. Now I never cook orecchiette any other way.

Using pre-diced ingredients means no extra chopping. And shiitake mushrooms have a particularly strong umami essence that I love in this dish, but what's most crucial is the garlic and herb goat cheese you stir in at the end. It creates a super slick and creamy sauce that melds all the flavors together.

1 To a very large sauté pan or pot over medium heat, add the pancetta. Cook for 5 minutes, stirring occasionally, then add 1 tablespoon of the olive oil and the mushrooms and cook for another 8 minutes, until the mushrooms and pancetta are crispy, stirring about once per minute to allow the mushrooms to crisp faster. Use a slotted spoon to transfer to a plate, then set aside.

2 To the pan, add the remaining tablespoon olive oil and the pasta. Cook for 2 to 3 minutes, stirring occasionally, until the orecchiette is slightly toasted and golden on the edges.

3 Add the chicken broth, 1 cup water, and a pinch of salt. Increase the heat to medium-high and simmer for 5 minutes, stirring frequently, then add the kale. Continue stirring for about 3 minutes until the pasta is cooked, the kale is wilted, and the broth is absorbed. If the liquid is absorbed before the pasta is fully cooked, add more water, ¼ cup at a time, until it is done.

4 Remove from the heat and stir in the goat cheese along with most of the pancetta and mushrooms. Season with salt and pepper to taste. Top with the reserved pancetta and mushrooms for a crispy garnish.

don't mess it up!

This pasta comes together quickly for a weeknight, but it does require some babysitting over the stove. Make sure to stir very frequently as it simmers—this will ensure all the pasta cooks evenly and none sticks to the bottom of the pan.

stuffing mac & cheese

The first time I posted a video for this recipe, I was falsely accused of "rage-baiting" by the Thanksgiving Side-Dish Police, so I must argue my case and plead not guilty. I make Stuffing Mac and Cheese for my holiday spread every year and have converted all the haters to true believers. Essentially, it combines two classic side dishes into one glorious creation. Rehydrated bread cubes toast and become a crunchy topping for the baked mac, which has provolone cheese for a sharp, nutty flavor. Pepperidge Farm is my favorite stuffing to use for this dish because the bread pieces are just the right size and it's already seasoned exactly to my liking.

prep time
10 minutes

cook time
45 minutes

yield
serves 8

- 4 cups herb-seasoned stuffing mix, such as Pepperidge Farm
- 4 tbsp melted salted butter
- ½ cup chicken or vegetable broth
- 8oz (225g) cheddar cheese, grated and divided
- 8oz (225g) provolone cheese, grated and divided
- 1lb (450g) fusilli or elbow pasta
- Two 12oz (354ml) cans evaporated milk
- 2 tsp Cajun seasoning, such as Tony's
- Chopped fresh sage, for garnish (optional)

1. Preheat the oven to 375°F (190°C). In a medium bowl, stir together the seasoned stuffing mix, butter, broth, and a small handful of each cheese.
2. To a large sauté pan or Dutch oven, add the pasta, evaporated milk, and 3 cups water. Bring to a boil over medium-high heat, stirring occasionally. Once simmering, reduce the heat to medium-low and cook for 10 minutes, stirring frequently, until the pasta is cooked.
3. Add the Cajun seasoning, then turn off the heat and add in the remaining cheeses, one handful at a time, stirring until melted. Remove from the heat and transfer to a 9 x 13-inch (22 x 33cm) baking dish.
4. Top the mac and cheese with the stuffing and bake for 30 minutes, until golden brown and bubbling on the sides. Let rest for 10 minutes and garnish with sage, if desired, before serving.

don't mess it up!

There's no other dish in which grating your own cheese is more crucial than with mac and cheese, because the anti-caking agent in pre-grated cheese will give you a clumpy bummer of a sauce. So get ready to use those muscles (or invest in a rotary grater, which I recently did, and it was an incredible decision).

use it up!

If you used fresh sage and have leftovers, try it in my Chicken Saltimbocca Gnocchi Skillet (page 137).

30ish minutes

no chop

one dish

italian beef & giardiniera pan pizza

prep time
5 minutes

cook time
15 minutes

yield
serves 4

2 tbsp olive oil, divided
1lb (450g) store-bought pizza dough
½ cup marinara sauce
2 tsp French onion soup mix, preferably Dan-O's
½ tsp garlic powder
½ tsp Italian seasoning
8 slices of provolone cheese
4 slices of deli roast beef
½ cup hot or mild giardiniera
½ cup sliced banana peppers
1 cup shredded mozzarella cheese

Watching *The Great British Bake Off* has instilled in me a fear of soggy bottoms, so here's my foolproof method for making pan pizza at home with a crust that would pass any Mary Berry inspection. While I've seen versions that require you to preheat the pan first, that is tempting the fate of scorched fingertips too much for my liking. Instead, I build the whole pizza in a cold oven-safe skillet, place it over high heat on the stovetop until you hear the dough crackling, then finish it in the oven. Any toppings you like will work, but this recipe is an ode to the city of Chicago's classic Italian beef sandwich—in pizza form. The French onion soup mix sprinkled on the dough evokes the flavor of the jus you would normally get on the sandwich, without adding any moisture to sog out the crust! Be sure to add lots of cheese all along the edges of the pan, which bakes into a crispy cheesy crust just like the pies at my favorite Chicago pizza place, Pequod's.

1. Preheat the oven to 475°F (240°C).
2. To a 12-inch (30cm) nonstick oven-safe skillet, add 1 tablespoon of the olive oil, then press out the pizza dough to fully cover the surface of the pan.
3. In a small bowl, stir together the remaining 1 tablespoon of olive oil with the marinara sauce, French onion mix, garlic powder, and Italian seasoning. Spread the sauce evenly on the dough then spread out the provolone cheese so it touches the edges of the pan. Top with the roast beef, giardiniera, banana peppers, and mozzarella.
4. Place the skillet on the stove over medium-high heat for 3 minutes, rotating the pan for an even cook and to get the bottom of the dough crispy.
5. Transfer to the oven and bake for 10 to 12 minutes, until the top of the pizza and the crust is golden brown.

use it up!

You'll probably have leftover French onion soup mix in the packet since you're just using a couple of teaspoons here, but don't toss it out! It is great mixed into burgers or meatballs and is awesome as a seasoning for my French Onion Steak Bites (page 168).

Gimme Pizza
Gimme Pizza
P-i-z-z-a

eggplant parm french bread pizza
porchetta-spiced sausage and broccolini rabe french bread pizza
buffalo chicken french bread pizza

porchetta-spiced sausage & broccoli rabe french bread pizza

I love playing with nostalgic concepts and merging them with my ever slightly more evolved adult palate. In that spirit, I give you (drumroll please) . . . my perfected French bread pizza method! This is a staple of many American childhoods. Unlike the name suggests, French bread is not the same thing as a French baguette, which will be too crunchy without enough surface area for toppings. Any loaf with a softer, wider, sturdy crust will do the trick.

The next three recipes use the same technique described below: pre-toasting the bread with garlic oil to form a sturdy foundation. Then you can switch up the sauces and toppings, depending on your mood. For this first recipe, I'm using spices and herbs you'd find in porchetta, an Italian slow-roasted pork shoulder, but with ground pork instead. Think of it like making your own Italian sausage spice blend. It's much faster than traditional porchetta but still pairs perfectly with broccoli rabe's slight bitterness and the sharp saltiness of fontina cheese.

prep time
10 minutes

cook time
20 minutes

yield
serves 4

- 12–14in (30–36cm) loaf of soft French or Italian bread, split in half lengthwise
- ¼ cup olive oil, divided
- 2 tsp garlic powder
- ½lb (225g) ground pork
- 1 small bunch of broccoli rabe, cut into bite-size pieces
- 1 tsp ground fennel
- 1 tbsp minced fresh rosemary, or 1 tsp dried rosemary
- ¾ tsp red pepper flakes
- Kosher salt and freshly ground black pepper, to taste
- Zest and juice of 1 lemon
- 1 cup marinara or vodka sauce
- 3 cups shredded fontina cheese

1. Preheat the oven to 375°F (190°C).
2. On a sheet pan, place both halves of the loaf, brush all over with 2 tablespoons of the olive oil, and sprinkle with the garlic powder. Bake for 8 minutes, until slightly browned and crunchy. Remove from the oven and adjust the temperature to broil.
3. Meanwhile, in a large skillet over medium-high heat, add the remaining 2 tablespoons olive oil and cook the pork for 6 minutes, until browned and crumbled into bite-size pieces.
4. Add the broccoli rabe, ground fennel, rosemary, and red pepper flakes. Season with salt and pepper to taste. Cook for another 4 minutes, until the broccolini is tender and bright green, then finish with the lemon zest and juice.
5. Spoon the marinara sauce on the bread and top with the sausage-and-broccoli-rabe mixture. Cover with the cheese and broil for 2 to 3 minutes, until melted and browned on top, watching carefully to make sure the pizza doesn't burn. Cut and serve.

simple shortcut

I like to add my own spices like fennel, rosemary, and pepper flakes to the pork to give it that porchetta-style flavor, but this is also fantastic simply using Italian sausage, which already has the seasonings in it.

30ish minutes

one dish

buffalo chicken french bread pizza

prep time
10 minutes

cook time
15 minutes

yield
serves 4

12–14in (30–36cm) loaf of soft French or Italian bread, split in half lengthwise
2 tbsp olive oil or melted butter
1 tsp garlic powder
4 cups diced or shredded rotisserie chicken (from 1 rotisserie chicken)
½ cup buffalo sauce
1 tbsp ranch seasoning, such as Hidden Valley
⅔ cup blue cheese crumbles
¼ cup chopped chives, divided
2 cups shredded mild cheddar cheese
Ranch dressing, to serve

For a really quick version of this recipe, I've used the store-bought buffalo-chicken dip from my local Publix, but it is a little more fun to make it yourself and control the ingredients that go in. That means blue cheese crumbles—and lots of 'em. The ranch seasoning adds a concentrated punch of zesty flavor that's reinforced with a little saucy ranch drizzle on top.

1. Preheat the oven to 375°F (190°C).
2. On a sheet pan, place both halves of the loaf, brush all over with the olive oil, and sprinkle with the garlic powder. Bake for 8 minutes, until slightly browned and crunchy. Remove from the oven and adjust the temperature to broil.
3. Meanwhile, in a bowl, stir together the chicken, buffalo sauce, ranch seasoning, blue cheese, and 2 tablespoons of the chives.
4. Divide the buffalo-chicken mixture over the bread and top with the cheddar cheese. Return to the oven and broil for 2 to 3 minutes, until melted, watching carefully so the pizza doesn't burn. Remove from the broiler, top with the remaining 2 tablespoons chives and a drizzle of ranch, then cut and serve.

use it up!

If you have leftover buffalo sauce, try it in my Nashville Hot Chicken and Pickle Dip (page 220) . . . It's like buffalo-chicken dip, but better, if that's possible.

eggplant parm french bread pizza

I never enjoyed eggplant Parmesan all that much until I ordered it as an appetizer on a trip to Naples. I learned that the more traditional Italian version isn't super heavy and deep fried with breadcrumbs, unlike its Italian American counterpart. The eggplant is simply sautéed or roasted with extra-virgin olive oil and sweet San Marzano tomatoes, then topped with mozzarella cheese and fresh basil. I pile that on French bread and call it a pizza, which I'm sure Neapolitans would take no issue with.

prep time
10 minutes

cook time
20 minutes

yield
serves 4

- 12–14in (30–36cm) loaf of soft French or Italian bread, split in half lengthwise
- ⅓ cup olive oil, divided
- 2 tsp garlic powder
- 1 small eggplant, about 1lb (450g), diced into ¼in pieces
- 2 cups halved cherry tomatoes (from 1 pint)
- ¾ cup marinara sauce
- Kosher salt, to taste
- 3 garlic cloves, minced
- ¼ cup torn fresh basil leaves, divided
- 6oz (170g) low-moisture mozzarella cheese, shredded (see note)
- ¼ cup grated Parmesan cheese

1. Preheat the oven to 375°F (190°C).
2. On a sheet pan, place both halves of the loaf, brush all over with half the olive oil, and sprinkle with the garlic powder. Bake for 8 minutes, until slightly browned and crunchy. Remove from the oven and switch temperature to broil.
3. Meanwhile, in a large skillet over medium-high heat, add the remaining olive oil and heat for 1 minute. Add the eggplant, tomatoes, marinara, and salt. Cook for 12 minutes, stirring frequently, until the eggplant is very soft and the tomatoes break down. Stir in the garlic and half the basil and cook for 1 more minute.
4. Divide the eggplant mixture over the bread and top with the cheeses. Return to the oven and broil for 2 to 3 minutes, until melted, watching carefully so the pizza doesn't burn. Top with the remaining basil, cut, and serve.

don't mess it up!

While I love a soft ball of fresh mozzarella on an eggplant Parmesan, for this recipe, it's important to go with the block of low-moisture mozzarella. You want that melty cheese, but the fresh mozzarella contains more water that releases and risks sogging out your crispy crust.

30ish minutes

6 ingredients

no chop

spinach & mushroom sheet-pan pizzadillas

prep time
10 minutes

cook time
20 minutes

yield
serves 6

- Twelve 6in (15cm) flour tortillas
- 3 cups shredded Italian cheese blend, such as mozzarella and fontina
- 4 tbsp olive oil, divided
- 5oz (140g) sliced cremini mushrooms
- 6oz (170g) bag fresh spinach
- 1 tsp garlic powder
- Kosher salt and freshly ground black pepper, to taste
- ½ cup marinara or vodka sauce

This one goes out to all those who have been following me since the first time I went viral for making a deep-fried pizzadilla recipe so bone-chillingly awful it made the national news. (If you have no idea what I'm talking about, I know you skipped past the introduction, but I forgive you. Catch up on page 17.) So I felt a moral obligation to redeem the pizzadilla in my book, no deep-frying required. As the title suggests, this is a vegetarian spinach-and-mushroom version, but once you learn the technique, you could mix it up with any toppings you prefer. The secret for success here is preheating the sheet pan so the tortillas get a nice bottom crust. Use this method any time you make a big batch of quesadillas for a crowd, so it all comes out hot at the same time! You can make this a no-chop recipe by buying pre-sliced cremini mushrooms.

1. Preheat the oven to 400°F (200°C). Place a large sheet pan in the oven while it preheats so it gets very hot.
2. Lay out 6 tortillas, sprinkle half the cheese among them, then cover each with another tortilla, for a total of 6 quesadillas.
3. Carefully take the hot pan out of the oven and brush the surface with 2 tablespoons of the olive oil, then add the quesadillas to the pan. Brush the tops with another tablespoon olive oil, then return the sheet pan to the oven to bake for 12 to 14 minutes, flipping halfway through, until the cheese is melted and the tortillas start to crisp. Remove the pan from the oven and adjust the temperature to broil.
4. Meanwhile, in a large skillet over medium-high heat, add the remaining tablespoon olive oil. Once shimmering, add the mushrooms and cook for 7 to 8 minutes, until browned. Then add the spinach and cook until just wilted. Add the garlic powder and season with salt and pepper to taste.
5. Onto each quesadilla, spoon the marinara, then top with the mushroom-and-spinach mixture and the remaining cheese. Broil for 3 to 4 minutes, until melted. Let cool for 3 minutes then cut them into quarters before serving.

A Shay's tape / Summer
STOP
FF
REW
PLAY
REC

30ish minutes

6 ingredients

one dish

muffin-tin pepperoni-jalapeño pizza rolls

Muffin-tin pizza rolls are another one of my most-viral recipes of all time. Many of my most popular dishes are made in a muffin tin, which is always fun for me as a developer: to find new uses for what seems like a single-purpose cooking vessel. This snack is ideal for the muffin-tin treatment, since each roll gets crispy cheesy edges that contrast its gooier center. I use Pillsbury Thin and Crispy Pizza Crust Dough because it's the perfect size for a standard 12-cup pan. I made them for the first time for Super Bowl LVIII, when the Kansas City Chiefs won and Taylor Swift rushed to the field after, so they always make my heart go pitter-patter.

prep time
15 minutes

cook time
15 minutes

yield
makes 12 rolls

Cooking spray or softened butter
8oz (226g) tube refrigerated pizza dough, preferably Pillsbury Thin and Crispy Pizza Crust Dough
⅓ cup marinara or vodka sauce, plus more to serve
1½ cups shredded mozzarella cheese
20 large pepperoni slices
1 large jalapeño, chopped
Ranch dressing, to serve (optional)

1. Preheat the oven to 450°F (230°C). Grease a 12-cup muffin tin with cooking spray.
2. On a clean kitchen surface or cutting board, roll out the dough into a 12 x 9-inch (30 x 22cm) rectangle. Top with the marinara sauce, cheese, pepperoni, and jalapeño. Gently roll the dough, starting from the longer side, to create a very tight log. Using a serrated knife, slice the dough into 12 rounds about 1 inch thick. They may be a bit messy, but they will come together as they bake.
3. Place the rolls in the muffin tin and bake for 12 to 15 minutes, until they are a deep golden brown and slightly caramelized around the edges. Use a knife to loosen them up around the edges, then transfer to a serving platter. Serve with more marinara and ranch dressing, if using.

don't mess it up!

Using a serrated bread knife is necessary to get clean, even slices for each round. Unless your chef's knife is very sharp, it will likely just smush it all down and the sauce and filling can fall out. (If this happens, just cobble it all together into the best roll you can to get it into the muffin tin—it will work itself out in the oven as long as all the ingredients are in there, it just might not be as beautiful.)

chicken dinners

30ish minutes

no chop

one dish

cheater's chicken parm

prep time
5 minutes

cook time
20 minutes

yield
serves 4

½ cup panko breadcrumbs
3 tbsp olive oil, divided
1 tsp garlic powder
1 tsp Italian seasoning
Kosher salt and freshly ground black pepper, to taste
3lb (1.35kg) boneless, skinless chicken breasts
24oz (680g) jar marinara, arrabbiata, or vodka sauce
¼ cup torn fresh basil leaves
4 slices of mozzarella or provolone cheese
½ cup grated Parmesan cheese

Let me introduce you to one of the first recipes I ever posted on social media that has become perhaps my most popular over the years. While I don't advocate being a cheater, sometimes it's acceptable in a more low-stakes scenario such as this one. You've got all the elements of a chicken parm—thinly sliced chicken breasts, gooey cheese, crunchy seasoned breadcrumbs all bubbling away in a red sauce—but simplified. And you'll achieve crunchiness, cheesiness, and sauciness without any frying involved. The trick is to let the chicken simmer in the sauce at the bottom of the pan. Herbed breadcrumbs go on top of the cheese, so there's no sogginess in sight. Call it deconstructed, reverse engineered, whatever you want—just be warned it will be on your weekly rotation based on many first-hand testimonies that slide into my DMs.

1 Preheat the broiler to low.

2 In a small bowl, combine the panko, 1 tablespoon of the olive oil, the garlic powder, Italian seasoning, and a pinch of salt and pepper. Stir to combine and set aside.

3 Heat a large oven-safe skillet over medium-high heat and add the remaining 2 tablespoons olive oil. Season the chicken with salt and pepper, then sear in the pan for 4 to 5 minutes per side—they do not need to be fully cooked through yet. Transfer to a plate.

4 Reduce the heat to medium-low and add the marinara sauce and half the basil to the same skillet. Return the chicken to the pan and cook for about 3 minutes until the sauce begins to bubble, then remove from the heat.

5 Top each chicken breast with the cheeses and the breadcrumb mixture. Broil for 3 minutes, or until the cheese is melted and the breadcrumbs are browned and crispy. Remove from the oven and garnish with the remaining basil before serving.

don't mess it up!

Every broiler is different, and most of them have hot spots that will brown the breadcrumbs faster in certain places. For dishes covered with cheese on top, even browning isn't as crucial, but burnt breadcrumbs are much more unpleasant—so be sure to check on it while it's under the broiler and rotate or move the pan as necessary.

30ish minutes

no chop

one dish

weeknight carnitas-style chicken tacos

Traditional carnitas call for cooking a big piece of pork low and slow, typically with fresh orange, garlic, bay leaf, and Mexican oregano. This can take all day to get tender, but really, step two—crisping the meat in a hot skillet—is the most important part. My weeknight-friendly recipe takes inspiration from the classic Mexican dish, substituting pork with shredded rotisserie chicken that I amp up with broth and orange juice. Adding spices during the crisping process pulls the robust flavors together. Warm the tortillas directly on the stovetop for 30 seconds per side for an extra touch of char.

prep time
10 minutes

cook time
10 minutes

yield
serves 4

2 tsp light or dark brown sugar
1½ tsp kosher salt
1 tsp garlic powder
1 tsp onion powder
1 tsp Mexican oregano
1 tsp cumin
3 tbsp neutral oil
4 cups shredded rotisserie chicken
2 tbsp freshly squeezed orange juice
⅓ cup chicken broth

to serve
Warm tortillas
Guacamole, pico de gallo, lime wedges, and any other desired toppings

1. In a small bowl, stir together the brown sugar, salt, garlic powder, onion powder, oregano, and cumin.
2. To a large nonstick skillet over medium-high heat, add the oil and heat until shimmering, then add the chicken and the seasoning blend. Cook for 6 minutes, or until a crust forms, taking care not to stir too much so caramelization forms on the pan.
3. Add the orange juice and chicken broth to deglaze the pan (see note on page 60), and cook for an additional 2 minutes, until the liquid is absorbed.
4. Serve with the warm tortillas and toppings of your choice.

ingredient intel

Mexican oregano differs greatly from standard oregano, as it's more pungent in flavor with citrus notes. It is (obviously) a staple in Mexican cooking and something I always keep on hand, but if you can't find it, standard oregano works in a pinch for this recipe. But in that case, I would add some of the zest from the orange (maybe 1 teaspoon) when you add the juice to punch up the citrus flavor.

skillet raclette chicken
with creamy leeks & mushrooms

prep time
10 minutes

cook time
28 minutes

yield
serves 4

- 1½ cups chicken broth
- ⅓ cup heavy cream
- 1 tbsp Dijon mustard
- 1 tbsp cornstarch
- 3lb (1.35kg) boneless, skinless chicken breasts
- 1 tbsp Cajun seasoning, such as Tony's
- 2 tbsp olive oil, divided
- 4oz (115g) diced pancetta
- 8oz (225g) cremini or mixed mushrooms, sliced
- 1 leek, halved lengthwise and thinly sliced (see note on page 135)
- 4 slices of raclette, Swiss, or Gruyère cheese
- Minced chives, for garnish (optional)
- Baguette, to serve (optional)

I like to think of this dish as a fancy version of one of my favorite chain-restaurant meals, the Alice Springs Chicken from Outback Steakhouse. It's a symphony of blackened chicken topped with mushrooms, bacon, and a blanket of cheddar cheese, and served with a honey-mustard sauce. Here, I use pancetta instead of bacon because I don't want the smoked flavor of bacon in this dish, then I simmer the chicken in a creamy Dijon sauce and melt a rich and nutty Swiss, raclette-style cheese on top. Okay, so it's really not much like the Outback version, but we can say it's an offspring that's just a little more elegant.

1. In a medium bowl or measuring cup, whisk together the broth, heavy cream, mustard, and cornstarch and set aside.
2. Pat the chicken dry with paper towels and coat with the Cajun seasoning. To a large skillet or sauté pan over medium-high heat, add 1 tablespoon of the olive oil and heat until shimmering. Cook the chicken for 5 minutes per side, until golden brown—it does not need to be fully cooked through yet. Transfer to a plate and set aside.
3. Reduce the heat to medium and add the remaining tablespoon olive oil to the pan along with the pancetta, mushrooms, and leek. Cook for 8 minutes, stirring occasionally, until the pancetta and mushrooms are slightly crispy and the leeks are softened.
4. Pour the chicken-broth mixture into the skillet, scraping up any browned bits from the bottom of the pan, then add the chicken back in, along with any juices from the plate.
5. Reduce the heat to medium-low and let simmer for 5 minutes. Spoon some of the sauce on top of the chicken and top each chicken breast with a slice of cheese. Cover with a lid and cook for 5 minutes, until the cheese is melted. Garnish with minced chives and serve with a torn baguette for dipping, if desired.

ingredient intel

Raclette is originally a Swiss dish that involves a wheel of bubbly, hot, gooey cheese that gets scraped onto bread, potatoes, or other various vegetables. Now, you'll find cheese at the supermarket labeled "raclette cheese," named so because it's melty, sharp, nutty, and ideal for this preparation. That's what I use for this dish, but you can also use plain old slices of Swiss cheese, and it will still be delicious.

keep it clean

Leeks are a milder alternative to onions and are absolutely delicious, but they do require a little more prep because they are grown in sandy soil and can therefore catch a lot of dirt. The best way to prep them is to cut off and discard the fibrous green top, then split them in half lengthwise and run the inside under cold tap water, making sure it gets into each layer to get all the dirt and grit out.

30ish minutes

one dish

chicken saltimbocca gnocchi skillet

Typical Roman saltimbocca features veal cutlets wrapped in prosciutto with fresh sage and cooked in a rich, buttery pan sauce. One of the first dishes I ever learned to cook was Chicken Saltimbocca, a recipe I saw on an episode of Rachael Ray's *30-Minute Meals*. I was immediately won over by how fast, easy, and exciting it was. Never would I have imagined that one day I'd work in Rachael's test kitchen, much less have a version in my own cookbook.

This twist on a twist is in the same spirit as Rachael's recipe, but swaps in diced chicken breast along with store-bought gnocchi for a heartier one-pot meal. It takes less than 30 minutes and is just as satisfying as my first saltimbocca experience years ago.

prep time
15 minutes

cook time
15 minutes

yield
serves 4

- 4 tbsp salted butter, divided
- 8oz (225g) boneless, skinless chicken breasts, diced
- Kosher salt and freshly ground black pepper, to taste
- 2oz (60g) prosciutto, about 3 slices, torn into bite-size pieces
- 6 sage leaves, sliced or left whole
- 1½ tsp flour
- 1 cup chicken broth
- 12oz (340g) bag refrigerated potato gnocchi
- 1 tbsp fresh lemon juice
- ¼ cup grated Parmesan cheese

1. In a large skillet or sauté pan over medium heat, melt 2 tablespoons of the butter, add the chicken, and season lightly with salt and pepper. Cook for 1 minute, then add the prosciutto and sage and cook for 5 minutes, stirring frequently. Use a slotted spoon to transfer everything to a plate.
2. In the same skillet, melt the remaining 2 tablespoons butter and cook for 3 minutes, stirring occasionally, until slightly browned and nutty, then immediately add the flour and whisk for another minute before pouring in the chicken broth. Bring to a boil to thicken, then add the gnocchi and reduce the heat to medium-low. Cover with a lid or aluminum foil and let cook for 5 minutes, stirring at least once to prevent it from sticking to the bottom, until the gnocchi is tender.
3. Return the chicken, prosciutto, and sage to the skillet along with any juices collected on the plate. Stir in the lemon juice and finish with the Parmesan.

don't mess it up!

Prosciutto is very salty, and that salt only concentrates as it crisps up in this recipe. Because of this, you shouldn't season chicken like you normally would. I recommend to go light at the beginning (½ teaspoon, tops), then add more at the end if needed.

6 ingredients

one dish

athenian chicken
with steak fries

prep time
10 minutes

cook time
1 hour

yield
serves 4–6

- 3lb (1.35kg) bone-in, skin-on chicken thighs
- Kosher salt and freshly ground black pepper, to taste
- ½ cup olive oil
- Zest and juice of 1 lemon, plus wedges to serve
- 2 tbsp red wine vinegar
- 3 tbsp chopped fresh oregano, or 1 tbsp dried oregano, plus more to serve
- 2 garlic cloves, grated or minced
- 28oz (793g) bag frozen steak fries

There's a Greek restaurant in Chicago called the Athenian Room, and they serve a dish called Chicken Kalamata Style, which is crispy-skin roasted chicken served atop a bed of steak fries that soak up all the drippings and the garlicky lemon-and-herb sauce. It's one of those dishes that's so simple but will haunt you eternally—in a good way. When I need to satisfy my craving for it in a pinch, I use a bag of frozen steak-cut fries crisped in the oven, and cook the chicken thighs right on top. The exposed parts of the fries get extra crispy, while the parts under the chicken soak up all the flavor. It's the one time in life when you actually want soggy fries, because those chicken juices are so damn good.

1. Preheat the oven to 350°F (180°C).
2. Season the chicken with salt and pepper to taste.
3. In a large bowl, whisk together the olive oil, lemon juice, vinegar, and oregano. Reserve ¼ cup of this marinade and, to it, add the garlic and lemon zest. Place the chicken in the bowl with the rest of the marinade and toss to coat. (You can also leave it covered in the refrigerator for up to 8 hours.)
4. In the bottom of a large casserole dish, arrange the fries in an even layer. Bake for 15 minutes, until crispy.
5. Place the chicken on top of the fries and pour any excess marinade from the bowl over top. Bake for 40 to 45 minutes, until cooked through and the chicken skin is crispy.
6. Remove from the oven and brush the chicken with a layer of the reserved marinade while it's hot. Serve with the lemon wedges and more oregano.

don't mess it up!

The reason I don't add the garlic and lemon zest to the marinade with the chicken before cooking is because they will burn in the oven, so instead I brush those flavors on at the very end, when the chicken is hot, for a fresh and delightfully pungent finish. The garlic will cook ever so slightly when it touches the heat from the chicken, so it will lose some of its harsh bite but still pack a punch of flavor.

30ish minutes

one dish

hoisin chicken lettuce wraps

One of the only bad things about living on an island that's 3½ hours away from the nearest city is the lack of proximity to my favorite chain restaurants (though we do, unsurprisingly, have a Margaritaville in Key West). That means I can't quite satisfy a craving for P. F. Chang's lettuce wraps in the urgent way I often need to. On the flip side, it's kind of awesome because I can take cues from what I love and customize a dish to my taste buds. For example, I'm not a big fan of water chestnuts, so I skip those and top with crushed peanuts instead for a superior crunch.

prep time
15 minutes

cook time
15 minutes

yield
serves 4

- 2 tbsp hoisin sauce, plus more to serve
- 2 tbsp sriracha
- 2 tbsp soy sauce
- 4 garlic cloves, grated or minced
- Juice of 1 lime
- 2 tsp neutral oil
- 1lb (450g) ground chicken or turkey
- Kosher salt, to taste
- 1 bunch of scallions, sliced, green and white parts separated
- ½ cup store-bought matchstick carrots, divided
- Romaine or butter lettuce leaves, to serve
- Crushed peanuts, to serve (optional)
- Sliced Fresno peppers, to serve (optional)

1. In a small bowl or measuring cup, stir together the hoisin sauce, sriracha, soy sauce, garlic, lime juice, and 1 tablespoon water. Set the sauce aside.
2. In a medium skillet, heat the oil over medium heat. Add the chicken and season lightly with salt. Cook for 8 to 10 minutes, crumbling the meat with the back of the spoon, until browned.
3. Add the whites of the scallions and cook for another 2 minutes, then pour in the sauce and stir to coat. Let simmer for 2 minutes. If it's looking dry, you can add a splash of water. Stir in half the carrots and cook till warmed through.
4. Remove from the heat and serve with the lettuce, remaining carrots, scallion greens, more hoisin sauce, and crushed peanuts and Fresno peppers, if using.

don't mess it up!

This is one of those recipes that can easily become too salty, since the sauce ingredients all contain a good amount of salt already. Go easy on the salt on the meat before you sauce it—you can always add more to taste at the end.

use it up!

If you have leftover matchstick carrots, use them in my Lemon Chicken Tortellini Soup (page 66) or my Thai Basil Red Curry (page 181). These are an awesome shortcut ingredient to use when you don't feel like chopping or shredding carrots!

braised chicken
with italian beans & greens

prep time
10 minutes

cook time
50 minutes

yield
serves 4–6

2lb (900g) boneless, skinless chicken thighs
Kosher salt and freshly ground black pepper, to taste
Two 15.5oz (439g) cans cannellini beans with the liquid
2 cups chopped escarole, kale, spinach or other leafy green
2 tsp Calabrian chili paste, or 1 tsp red pepper flakes
Zest and juice of 1 lemon
3 garlic cloves, grated or minced
¾ cup chicken broth
2 tbsp cornstarch
3 tbsp extra-virgin olive oil
Crusty bread, to serve

There's a whole category of recipes that I internally call "dippin' dinners," which basically entails throwing everything in one pan, letting it all bake together in a flavor-packed sauce, then serving it straight out of the pan with crusty bread for—you guessed it—dippin'! Perhaps one day I'll make a whole cookbook of dippin' dinners, but for now, here's my take on Italian white beans braised with greens, adding chicken for a more complete meal. Using thighs allows this dish to cook for long enough to develop a robust sauce without drying out the chicken. Plus, the extra fat lends more complexity to the sauce, so don't be tempted to swap in chicken breasts . . . Dippin' dinners are not the time to go lean.

1. Preheat the oven to 350°F (180°C).
2. Pat the chicken dry with paper towels and season with salt and pepper.
3. To a 9 x 13-inch (22 x 33cm) casserole dish, add the beans with the liquid, the leafy greens, chili paste, lemon zest and half the juice, and garlic. In a measuring cup, whisk together the broth and cornstarch and add it to the dish. Season with salt and pepper to taste, stir to combine, and nestle the chicken in the pan.
4. Drizzle the olive oil over everything and cover with aluminum foil. Bake for 25 minutes. Remove the foil and bake for another 25 minutes. Squeeze in the remaining lemon juice, and serve with the crusty bread on the side for dipping.

use it up!

If you have leftover Calabrian chili paste, use it in my Mascarpone Rigatoni alla Vodka (page 102), my Honeymoon Choripán (page 89), or my Parmesan Pork Chops with Calabrian Chili Cauliflower (page 152).

chicken chili tot pie

The first time I ever called something a "tot pie" and posted it online, I quickly learned that the phrase "Minnesota Nice" does not mean that people from Minnesota are nice; it means they will absolutely tear you to shreds in the politest way possible. You see, in Minnesota, a casserole topped with tater tots is called hot dish, and calling it anything else can cause a frenzy. I think "tot pie" is more fun to say, so I'm gonna risk it again. This version is basically like upside-down chili-cheese tots, which was the alternate title I had for the recipe, but ultimately, I want to bait the Minnesotans . . . lovingly.

prep time
15 minutes

cook time
1 hour

yield
serves 4–6

1 tbsp olive oil or neutral oil
1 large yellow onion, chopped
2 medium poblano peppers, chopped
Kosher salt, to taste
1lb (450g) ground chicken or turkey
1 tsp garlic powder
1 tbsp ancho chili powder
15.5oz (439g) can spicy chili beans with juices
28oz (794g) can diced tomatoes with green chiles
1lb (450g) frozen tater tots
8oz (227g) block sharp cheddar cheese, shredded
Your favorite chili toppings, such as diced raw onion, pickled jalapeños, cilantro, sour cream, and more cheese

1. Preheat the oven to 375°F (190°C).
2. To a large oven-safe skillet or a sauté pan over medium heat, add the oil, onion, and poblanos and season with salt to taste. Cook for 6 to 8 minutes, until the onion is slightly softened.
3. Add the chicken, garlic powder, and chili powder and cook for 6 minutes, crumbling the meat with the back of a spoon or a potato masher (see note below), until browned. Add the beans and tomatoes and let simmer for another 10 minutes, then remove from the heat. Season with more salt to taste.
4. Top with the frozen tater tots and transfer to the preheated oven. Bake for 25 minutes, until crispy. Top with the cheddar and return to the oven for another 8 to 10 minutes, until the cheese is melted and bubbling around the edges. Serve with your desired toppings.

equipment intel

I like a fine mince on the ground meat for chili, which can be hard to achieve with lean poultry because it tends to clump together in larger chunks. My favorite tool to break it up is a potato masher! Simply let the meat brown first and start to break it up with a wooden or silicon spoon, then switch to the masher and put some elbow grease into it.

ingredient intel

I always use ancho chili powder when making chili because it's made from pure dried poblano chiles and lends a consistently deep, smoky, just-slightly-spicy flavor. Regular chili powder varies much more greatly from brand to brand and is usually a mix of various spices, but it works here in a pinch! For other ways to use ancho chili powder, try my Choriqueso Enchilada Casserole (page 160), Cherry Cola Ribs (page 167), or Chili-Lime Corn & Black Bean Tacos (page 197).

30ish minutes

6 ingredients

no chop

one dish

grilled tuscan-esque chicken

with charred lemon

prep time
5 minutes

cook time
20 minutes

yield
serves 4

10oz (285g) jar sundried tomato pesto, divided
1 tbsp olive oil, plus more for drizzling
2lb (900g) boneless, skinless chicken thighs
2 tsp garlic powder
Kosher salt and freshly ground black pepper, to taste
1 lemon, halved
5oz (140g) arugula

I'm not sure when all chicken dishes using sundried tomatoes became labeled "Tuscan" in the US, and I'm sure the people of Tuscany would take umbrage, but it's a word association I can't shake. Let's just say this is a Tuscan-ish take on grilled chicken. A jar of store-bought sundried tomato pesto (I use the Flora brand) does all the heavy lifting and, when tossed with chicken thighs, makes for a quick but powerful marinade. Keep a bit of that marinade on the side to use as a bright finishing sauce. On the grill or grill pan, the natural sugars in the tomatoes caramelize and deepen the flavor. One bite, and suddenly I'm Diane Lane, freshly divorced but picking up the pieces under the Tuscan sun.

1. Preheat a grill or grill pan to medium-high.
2. To a large bowl, add about ¾ of the jar of pesto; reserve the rest for serving. Add the olive oil and stir, then add the chicken and coat evenly.
3. Season the chicken with the garlic powder, salt, and pepper. Grill for 6 to 7 minutes per side, until charred and cooked through, brushing any excess pesto from the bowl onto the chicken as it grills. Transfer to a platter and let rest for 5 minutes.
4. While the chicken is resting, place the lemon cut-side down on the grill or grill pan for 2 to 3 minutes, until charred. Top the chicken with the remaining pesto from the jar and drizzle with olive oil. Serve on a platter with the arugula and charred lemon.

use it up!

If you have leftover arugula, use it all up easily in my Whipped Ricotta Dip with Pistachio-Artichoke Pesto (page 206), or go the brunch route with my Smoked Salmon and Avocado Croissants (page 46).

don't mess it up!

If you're using an outdoor grill instead of a grill pan, you always want to have one hot side of the grill and one cool side of the grill, and that's particularly true for this recipe because the oil in the pesto can cause the grill to flare up a bit too much, and you'll end up with burnt chicken instead of beautifully charred chicken. If the chicken starts to get engulfed in flames, you'll want to move it immediately to the cooler side of the grill while you let the fire subside—it's for this reason that I generally recommend going with a grill pan if you're new to the world of grilling and want to ensure perfection in this recipe.

no chop

one dish

chicken enchilada tamale pie

In this house, we believe that box corn-muffin mix is better than 97 percent of homemade cornbread recipes. It doesn't dry out, it takes less than a minute to come together, and you can doctor it up however you like. Adding a can of diced green chiles and cheddar cheese to the mix makes this version a sibling to tamale pie, a staple from my Texas childhood that usually involves a slow-simmered beef chili at the bottom of the pan baked with crispy cornbread on top. The chicken enchilada version, however, requires no simmering and is cooked straight in the serving pan. Before you know it, you've got a hearty, delicious weeknight dinner.

prep time
10 minutes

cook time
40 minutes

yield
serves 6–8

4 cups shredded rotisserie chicken
10oz (283g) can red enchilada sauce
15.5oz (439g) can kidney chili beans with sauce
14.5oz (411g) can fire-roasted tomatoes
2 tbsp apple cider vinegar
3 tsp garlic powder, divided
Kosher salt, to taste
8.5oz (240g) box corn muffin mix, such as Jiffy
1 cup shredded mild cheddar cheese
4oz (113g) can diced green chiles
1 egg

1. Preheat the oven to 375°F (190°C).
2. To a 9 x 13-inch (22 x 33cm) casserole dish or 3.5-quart (3.3L) round baking dish, add the chicken, enchilada sauce, beans with sauce, tomatoes, vinegar, 1½ teaspoons of the garlic powder, and salt and stir to combine.
3. To a medium bowl, add the corn muffin mix, cheese, green chiles, egg, the remaining 1½ teaspoons garlic powder, and ⅓ cup water. Stir thoroughly to combine, then spread on top of the chicken mixture.
4. Bake for 35 to 40 minutes, until golden brown and bubbling around the edges.

use it up!

If you are looking for other ways to use apple cider vinegar, try out my tangy Pulled Pork Tostadas (page 156), my Honey-Dijon Praline Bacon (page 46), or my Bologna Sandwiches Au Cheval (page 90).

the other meats

30ish minutes

6 ingredients

one dish

james' favorite parmesan pork chops

with calabrian chili cauliflower

prep time
10 minutes

cook time
20 minutes

yield
serves 4

- 16oz (450g) cauliflower florets, or 1 large head of cauliflower cut into florets
- ¼ cup olive oil, divided
- Kosher salt and freshly ground black pepper, to taste
- 4 bone-in pork chops, about 1½in (3.5cm) thick
- 2 tbsp Dijon mustard
- ⅓ cup freshly grated Parmesan cheese
- 1 tbsp Calabrian chili paste
- 2 tbsp chopped fresh parsley

This is my husband's most requested meal, which is super chill for me because it's also one of the easiest in my repertoire. The biggest risk is overcooking the pork chops, which can truly dry out in a matter of minutes. My go-to cooking time for standard 1½-inch-thick bone-in pork chops is exactly 18 minutes (for this one, I broil the last couple of minutes to get a browned crust on top), then give it a 5-minute rest to make sure it's juicy. And I always make a little extra of the flavored oil I toss the cauliflower in for serving (sauce is always a good insurance policy in case the pork does get a little overcooked).

1. Preheat the oven to 425°F (220°C).
2. To a large sheet pan, add the cauliflower, toss with 1 tablespoon of the olive oil, and season with salt and pepper to taste.
3. Pat the pork chops dry with paper towels and season with salt and pepper to taste. Brush the top of the pork chops with the Dijon mustard, add to the sheet pan nestled in between the cauliflower, and sprinkle the Parmesan over top.
4. Bake for 15 minutes, then adjust the temperature to broil. Cook for another 2 to 3 minutes, until the pork chops are browned. Remove from the oven and let rest for 5 minutes.
5. Meanwhile, in a small bowl, stir together the remaining 3 tablespoons olive oil with the chili paste and parsley, and season with salt and pepper. Toss half this mixture with the cauliflower from the sheet pan. Arrange on a platter with the pork chops and serve with the remaining flavored oil on the side or drizzled on the pork chops.

ingredient intel

I'm totally not above buying powdery pre grated Parmesan cheese, but for this recipe, I really like it freshly grated for that sharp, nutty flavor to stand up to the tang of the mustard. The best way to grate a whole block of Parmesan quickly is to cut it into pieces and throw it in the food processor fitted with a standard blade, then let it rip.

Friend

Go for the Gusto

hard cider–braised brats
with cheddar pretzel buns

Being married to a Milwaukee-born man meant I had to do a lot of consulting and taste testing, and have some hard conversations before comfortably publishing this recipe with his approval. Bratwursts are an iconic Milwaukeean specialty, popularized by German immigrants who arrived there in the 1800s. And they're one of the very few dishes my husband has ever cooked for me, so he's kind of dramatic about them. His classic method involves boiling the brats in beer before charring them on the grill and serving them simply on a bun with sauerkraut and mustard. I'm less precious. Searing first, then braising the links in the same pan with the sliced onions will make them juicier. Swapping beer for hard apple cider offers a slightly sweet, fall-flavored twist. Then serve the brats with braised onions and pickled jalapeños or relish, nestled on a cheddar-coated pretzel bun. So in short, I completely changed his recipe, but mine is better, and he agrees.

prep time
15 minutes

cook time
35 minutes

yield
makes 6 sandwiches

2 tsp neutral oil
6 bratwursts
2 medium white onions, sliced
Kosher salt, to taste
12oz (354ml) bottle hard cider, such as Angry Orchard
6 soft pretzel sausage buns, such as the Pretzilla brand, split down the middle
12 slices of sharp cheddar cheese
Chopped pickled jalapeños or pickle relish, to serve

1. Preheat the broiler to low.
2. To a large skillet over medium-high heat, add the oil and heat for 2 minutes, until shimmering. Sear the bratwursts evenly for 3 minutes, then add the onions to the pan and cook, stirring occasionally, for another 8 minutes, until slightly softened. Season with salt to taste.
3. Add the cider and bring to a boil, then reduce the heat to a simmer and cook for 20 minutes, flipping the bratwursts halfway through, until the onions are cooked down and the liquid has reduced.
4. Meanwhile, put the buns on a sheet pan and lay 2 slices of cheese inside each roll. Broil for 2 to 3 minutes, until the cheese is just melted. Add the brats to the buns and top with the braised onions and the jalapeños and/or pickle relish.

use it up!

If you're looking for other recipes to use up the jar of chopped pickled jalapeños, try my Jalapeño Popper Hot Crab Dip (page 219) or use them in the dressing for my Tex-Mex Chopped Salad (page 70).

no chop

one dish

pulled pork tostadas
with ranch slaw

prep time
10 minutes

cook time
2½ hours

yield
makes 8 tostadas

- 2 cups chicken broth
- ½ cup ketchup
- ½ cup honey mustard, preferably the Maille brand
- ¼ cup plus 1 tbsp apple cider vinegar, divided
- 2 tbsp Worcestershire sauce
- 1 tbsp smoked paprika
- 1½lb (680g) cubed pork stew meat, such as pork shoulder
- Kosher salt and freshly ground black pepper, to taste
- 10oz (283g) bag slaw mix
- ¼ cup ranch dressing
- 8 tostadas, tortillas, or sandwich buns

As a Texan, I adore barbecue but have very little patience for perfecting the art of Texas craft barbecue—which generally involves days of dry rubbing and slow smoking over mesquite wood (not to mention years and years of practice). While the flavor and texture of a good smoked brisket can't be pulled off in any indoor kitchen, I've found that pulled pork is a more forgiving endeavor, since you're ultimately shredding and smothering the meat in sauce anyway. Braising pork shoulder in a vinegar-forward, slightly sweet concoction allows the flavors to concentrate as the meat slowly braises in the oven. I serve this on tostadas with a crunchy, Tex-Mex ranch slaw (I love Ken's steakhouse-style dressing) that contrasts with the melt-in-your-mouth pork. Any leftover slaw is also great on sandwiches and tacos.

1. Preheat the oven to 325°F (160°C).
2. In a medium oven-safe dish, whisk together the broth, ketchup, mustard, ¼ cup of the vinegar, the Worcestershire sauce, and paprika. Add the pork, cover with a lid or aluminum foil, and bake for 1 hour. Uncover and bake for another 1½ hours, or until the pork shreds easily with a fork.
3. Remove from the oven and use tongs or two forks to shred the pork; stir in the remaining 1 tablespoon vinegar, then season with salt and pepper to taste.
4. In a medium bowl, combine the slaw mix and the ranch dressing. Serve the pork on the tostadas, topped with the slaw.

use it up!

If you have extra tostadas, you can break them up into pieces and use them in place of the Fritos in my Fritos Migas Breakfast Tacos (page 36) or my Tex-Mex Chopped Salad (page 70).

30ish minutes

one dish

italian unstuffed-pepper casserole

Stuffed peppers are one dish you will never find in my dinner rotation. Why take the time to make a filling, pack it all inside some hollowed-out peppers, and bake it on a separate pan when you could simply . . . add those peppers to the stuffing, cover it all with cheese, and retain the same flavors in a fraction of the time with only one dish to clean up after? That also means using frozen rice to speed up your prep time (I think the P. F. Chang's brand is pretty great). Work smarter, not harder, my friends.

prep time
10 minutes

cook time
20 minutes

yield
serves 6

- 2 tbsp olive oil
- 1lb (450g) hot or mild Italian sausage, casings removed
- 2 red bell peppers, chopped
- 1 red onion, chopped
- 1 tbsp Italian seasoning
- 3 garlic cloves, grated or minced
- Kosher salt, to taste
- 2 cups cooked rice (I use thawed frozen rice)
- 1½ cups passata
- 6oz (170g) bag fresh spinach
- 2 cups shredded mozzarella or Italian cheese blend

1. Preheat the broiler to low.
2. To a large oven-safe sauté pan or round casserole dish over medium heat, add the oil and sausage and cook for 8 minutes, until browned.
3. Add the bell peppers, onion, Italian seasoning, garlic, and salt and cook for another 5 minutes.
4. Stir in the rice, passata, and 1 cup water. Add the spinach in batches until wilted. Taste and season with more salt if desired.
5. Top with the cheese and broil for 5 minutes, watching carefully, until melted and bubbly.

ingredient intel

Almost all Italians would scoff at the idea of "Italian seasoning," which is merely a blend of dried herbs like basil, oregano, thyme, and rosemary. I get it—it's not an actual "ingredient" they use in Italy, where fresh herbs reign supreme. It is, however, common in Italian American cooking, and when I think of classic Italian sausage and peppers you might find at a street fair here in the US, it's gotta have Italian seasoning, so for me, it's really necessary to evoke those flavors in this dish. For other ways to use it, try my Cheater's Chicken Parm (page 130), Laze-agna (page 110), or Chopped Italiano Sliders (page 207).

30ish minutes

no chop

one dish

choriqueso enchilada casserole

prep time
5 minutes

cook time
30 minutes

yield
serves 4–6

1 tsp neutral oil
1½lb (680g) Mexican chorizo
2 tsp ancho chili powder
1 tsp onion powder
Kosher salt and freshly ground black pepper, to taste
8oz (227g) block cream cheese
16oz (454g) jar salsa verde
10oz (283g) can red enchilada sauce
¼ cup fresh cilantro leaves, plus more to serve
8 corn tortillas, torn into pieces
8oz (225g) pepper jack or Monterey Jack cheese, grated

As much as I love the wow factor of pulling out a piping-hot tray of immaculately rolled enchiladas, most of the time, if I'm craving this dish, I make them in a pared-down way. Cook your filling ingredients in a skillet, add any spices you want (in this case, the chorizo is chockful of flavor so you don't need to add too much extra), pour in a jar of salsa, then tear up the tortillas into small pieces and throw them in. Cover with cheese before baking for a queso fundido vibe, and you're good as gold. It's minimal fuss and effort, and your taste buds will never know the difference.

1. Preheat the oven to 425°F (220°C).
2. To a large oven-safe skillet or sauté pan over medium heat, add the oil and chorizo, and cook for 8 minutes, or until browned and crumbled. Add the chili powder, onion powder, and salt and pepper to taste, and cook for 2 more minutes. Transfer a large spoonful of the meat to a small bowl for garnish.
3. Stir in the cream cheese, salsa verde, enchilada sauce, cilantro, and tortillas. Simmer for 3 minutes, then remove from the heat and cover with cheese.
4. Bake for 15 minutes, or until browned and bubbly. Garnish with reserved chorizo and more cilantro and let rest for 10 minutes before serving.

use it up!

If you have leftover cilantro, use it in the mango salsa for my Sweet-Heat Island Dogs (page 216), or blend the rest of the bunch into the Avocado-Jalapeño Ranch salad dressing (page 70) or the Green Godd-ish dressing (page 73).

EXTRA

spanish chorizo & swiss chard paella

Cooking paella is a similar technique to risotto (see page 185), but without all the stirring because, in this case, you don't want to release too much starch from the rice. This version is so easy as you don't need any special ingredients and everything cooks at roughly the same rate (unlike many seafood paellas where you have to add different ingredients at different times). Additionally, you don't need special equipment like a paella pan. I love a cast-iron skillet here, but any trusty skillet will do!

The trickiest part is actually the most important part: creating what's called the socarrat, a crusty layer of rice at the bottom of the pan that's a hallmark of any true Spanish paella. To make that happen, crank up the heat during the last 5 minutes of cooking. When you smell it just starting to burn, you know it's done. I know that may sound a bit scary, to intentionally burn your dish, so I have an alternative (see note below). Either way, don't worry. Your paella will not be ruined, and the crispy bottom bits will give a nice charred flavor and textural contrast once you plate it up.

prep time
15 minutes

cook time
45 minutes

yield
serves 4

- 1 tbsp olive oil
- 6oz (170g) Spanish chorizo, sliced
- 1 bunch of Swiss chard, stems diced and leaves roughly chopped
- 1 bunch of scallions, sliced, green and white parts separated
- 1 red pepper, diced
- 1 tsp turmeric (optional, see note below)
- Kosher salt and freshly ground black pepper, to taste
- 1½ cups short grain white rice
- 3 garlic cloves, grated or minced
- 4 cups (1 qt) chicken broth
- 1 tbsp sherry vinegar or red wine vinegar
- 2 tsp lemon juice

1. To a large skillet or sauté pan over medium heat, add the oil and chorizo and cook for 7 minutes, until crispy. Add the Swiss chard stems, scallion whites, red pepper, and turmeric, if using. Season lightly with salt and pepper to taste. Cook for 2 minutes, stirring frequently.
2. Add the rice and garlic and toast for 2 minutes, then add the chicken broth and 1 cup water. Bring to a simmer and cook for 18 minutes, stirring occasionally, until the rice is almost cooked through.
3. Stir in the vinegar and Swiss chard leaves and cook for 5 more minutes, until wilted. (If it looks dry and all the liquid is absorbed into the rice already, add another ½ cup water before moving on to the next step.)
4. Increase the heat to high and cook, without stirring, for another 5 to 7 minutes to form a crust on the bottom of the paella. Finish with lemon juice and serve garnished with the scallion greens.

ingredient intel

Most traditional Spanish paellas get their beautiful golden yellow from saffron, but that's a quite expensive ingredient that I don't keep on hand very often. Turmeric is a great substitute if you want to achieve that same look, and though the flavor is not quite the same, it does have similar earthy and floral notes. Feel free to use saffron instead if you want to get spendy!

hot tip

If you're not comfortable with the almost-burning method, finish the dish by placing the skillet under the broiler on high for 3 minutes. This will form a crust on the top of the paella as opposed to the bottom. Be sure to keep your eye on it!

30ish minutes

one dish

crispy beef & mushroom sheet-pan fajitas

prep time
15 minutes

cook time
20 minutes

yield
serves 4

1lb (450g) sliced beef fajita meat, preferably top round
1 tbsp Worcestershire sauce
1 tbsp chipotle hot sauce
Juice of 1 lime
¼ tsp baking soda
2 tbsp fajita or taco seasoning blend, divided
2 medium bell peppers, sliced
2 portobello mushrooms, sliced
1 red onion, cut into thick slices
2 tbsp neutral oil
Kosher salt, to taste
Tortillas, to serve
Fajita toppings, such as cheese, salsa, sour cream, or guacamole, to serve

No restaurant meal brings more dramatic flair than a sizzling skillet of fajitas arriving at the table. While I live for those theatrics, I save them for when I'm out. At home, I throw everything on a sheet pan, and let it rip in the oven. But here's the problem that plagues many sheet-pan fajita recipes: The meat and veggies crowd the pan and end up steaming instead of getting crispy and sizzling. That's why I add a little baking soda to the beef. This raises the meat's pH level, which breaks down the protein and facilitates browning. Who am I, Bill Nye?

1. Preheat the oven to 425°F (220°C).
2. To a medium bowl, add the beef, Worcestershire sauce, hot sauce, lime juice, baking soda, and 1 tablespoon of the seasoning blend, and stir to combine. Let sit for 10 minutes.
3. On a large sheet pan, add the peppers, mushrooms, and onion and toss everything with the oil and the remaining 1 tablespoon of the seasoning blend (see note below). Arrange with the beef in one even layer and sprinkle with salt to taste (if your seasoning blend is already salty, you can skip this).
4. Bake for 20 minutes, until cooked through and crispy. Serve with the tortillas and toppings.

equipment intel

For this recipe, I use a three-quarter sheet pan that is 21 x 15 inches. This is the perfect size for all the ingredients to fit in one even layer, but if you only have smaller half sheet pans, you should divide everything between two so the veggies have more surface area to crisp up.

6 ingredients

no chop

cherry cola ribs

My first experience combining meat and sugary soda came at a young age, when I used to go deer hunting with my dad and his friends. Every night, they would take all the venison we got from the day and marinate it overnight in Coca-Cola. Then we'd grill the meat for dinner the next evening. Real talk: I found the whole experience nauseating, but I've since come to appreciate it from a culinary standpoint. The acidity in the soda helped tenderize the lean deer meat, and the caramelization tamed any gaminess during the cooking process. Nowadays, I skip the venison and opt for a cherry-coke barbecue sauce, which is particularly exquisite on grilled pork ribs.

Regardless of how you prep and sauce the ribs, though, this foolproof method makes the meat fall off the bone every time: Start with a dry rub in the oven and cover with foil to lock in moisture; once the ribs are tender, char on the grill for that smoky-sweet flavor. Broiling is a great alternative if you can't fire up the grill.

prep time
10 minutes

cook time
2¼ hours

yield
serves 6

- 3lb (1.35kg) pork back ribs, about 2 racks, membrane removed or scored with a knife
- 1 tbsp ancho chili powder
- 1 tbsp smoked paprika
- Kosher salt and freshly ground black pepper, to taste
- 1½ cups barbecue sauce, such as Stubb's spicy sauce, plus more for serving
- 20fl oz (591ml) bottle cherry cola
- 4 corn cobs, grilled, to serve

1. Preheat the oven to 300°F (150°C).
2. Pat the ribs dry with paper towels and place them on a large rimmed sheet tray. Season with the chili powder, paprika, salt, and pepper and pat the seasoning into the meat. Add 1 cup water to the bottom of the pan, cover with aluminum foil, and bake for 2 hours.
3. Meanwhile, in a large saucepan over medium-high heat, add the barbecue sauce and cherry cola. Bring to a boil, then reduce the heat to medium and let simmer for 15 minutes, until reduced by half and thickened.
4. Heat a grill over medium-high or preheat the broiler to high. Brush the ribs with the cola barbecue sauce on both sides and grill or broil for 10 minutes, flipping once, until charred on each side. Serve with the corn and more barbecue sauce.

what's the deal with the membrane?

One big debate about ribs is whether to remove the thin membrane on the back of the bones, which can have a chewy texture and prevent the sauce from penetrating the meat. My grocery store removes the back membrane of the ribs for me, which is amazing—so always ask if they can do that. Otherwise, you can score it with a knife by making shallow cuts so the membrane will shrink up as it cooks and the sauce can hit the meat.

make it ahead

Once you've gotten past step three, you can store the covered ribs and barbecue sauce separately in the refrigerator for up to 2 days. When you want to serve them, just fire up the grill, cook as directed, and finish with the barbecue sauce.

french onion steak bites
with blue cheese wedges

prep time
15 minutes

cook time
15 minutes

yield
serves 4

- 1 head of iceberg lettuce, cut into 8 wedges
- 2 cups chopped cherry tomatoes (from 1 pint)
- 6 radishes, sliced
- ½ cup blue cheese crumbles
- ¼ cup chopped chives, divided
- 2 tsp neutral oil
- 1½lb (680g) tri-tip steak, cut into 1in (2.5cm) cubes
- 5 tbsp salted butter
- 1 tbsp French onion seasoning, preferably Dan-O's
- 4 garlic cloves, grated or minced
- Dressing, such as blue cheese, to serve

To me, the perfect steakhouse meal involves French Onion Soup, a sizzling buttery steak, and a crisp wedge salad, so this is like all of those flavors in one much more affordable weeknight dinner. Tri-tip is one of those cuts of meat that I'm almost tempted to gatekeep because it's affordable and doesn't require a long cooking time. While it doesn't have the marbled quality of, say, a ribeye, it's fantastic in this dish. With a quick sauté, the beef stays tender, and you'll get all the richness you need from the butter.

1. On a large platter, arrange the iceberg lettuce wedges and top with the tomatoes, radishes, blue cheese, and half the chives. Place in the refrigerator while you cook the steak.
2. To a medium skillet over medium-high heat, add the oil. Once shimmering, add the steak, and cook undisturbed for 3 to 4 minutes to form a crust. Stir, then add the butter and French onion seasoning, and reduce the heat to medium. Cook for another 5 to 7 minutes, stirring occasionally, until browned all over.
3. Add the garlic and the remaining chives, then immediately remove from the heat and stir for 30 seconds.
4. Drizzle your dressing of choice over the salad, and serve alongside the steak bites.

don't mess it up!

When you're adding minced garlic to a pan that's already this hot, it can easily burn to oblivion in seconds . . . and taint all this beautiful beef. That's why you have to kill the heat as soon as you add the garlic, making sure to stir and remove it from the stove immediately.

diy dressing

If you want to whip up your own quick blue cheese vinaigrette, add 4 ounces (115g) of blue cheese crumbles to a small food processor with ¼ cup olive oil, ¼ cup milk, 1 tablespoon of white wine vinegar, and a pinch of black pepper; process until smooth.

30ish minutes

6 ingredients

lamb chops
with feta & mint orzo salad

Lamb chops are one of those foods that feel super fancy and impressive but are shockingly easy to cook. They're so naturally flavorful that they don't require any seasoning besides salt and pepper (plus a little squeeze of lemon to cut the fat). It's vital, though, to sear them over high heat for a few minutes on each side to get a solid crust. I like them on the rarer side, but even if you overcook them a bit, the flavors will still shine. Serve with a simple 5-ingredient orzo salad, which can be conveniently made ahead and includes one of my favorite pantry ingredients: marinated feta. I use the Castello brand, oil and all, which is packed with herbs and spices, offering a flavorful shortcut for an elegant summer dinner ready in under 30 minutes.

prep time
10 minutes

cook time
20 minutes

yield
serves 4

1½ cups orzo, cooked according to package instructions, rinsed until cool
9⅓oz (265g) jar marinated feta, marinating oil reserved
2 cups chopped cherry tomatoes (from 1 pint)
⅔ cup chopped fresh mint, plus more to serve
Zest and juice of 1 lemon, plus wedges to serve
2 tsp neutral oil
2lb (900g) lamb chops
Kosher salt and freshly ground black pepper, to taste

1. To a large bowl, add the orzo, marinated feta and marinating oil, tomatoes, mint, lemon zest, and half the lemon juice. Place in the refrigerator while you cook the lamb chops.
2. To a large skillet or grill pan over high heat, add the oil. Pat the lamb chops dry with a paper towel and season with salt and black pepper to taste. Once the oil is shimmering, add the lamp chops and cook for 4 minutes per side, until a deep golden brown. Work in 2 batches if necessary so as not to overcrowd the pan.
3. Serve on a platter with the orzo salad, lemon wedges, and mint.

make it ahead

The orzo salad can be fully made the day before—and only gets better with time! So if you're having a summertime dinner party or cookout, all you have to do on the day of is sear or grill the lamb chops and pour the wine.

use it up!

If you have leftover mint, try it in my Tabbouleh with Spiced Chickpeas (page 193).

lebanese beef & green beans

prep time
20 minutes

cook time
2¼ hours

yield
serves 4

1 tbsp neutral oil
1½lb (680g) beef stew meat, such as boneless chuck, thinly sliced or cubed
1½ tsp ground coriander
1½ tsp ground cumin
Kosher salt and freshly ground black pepper, to taste
1 white onion, chopped
1 cup beef broth, plus more as needed
2½ cups passata
2 cinnamon sticks, or 1 tsp ground cinnamon
12oz (340g) green beans, ends trimmed
Warm pita, to serve

[Alexa, play "Cinnamon Girl" by Lana del Rey.]

When I was growing up, the scent of cinnamon wafted from our kitchen on a daily basis—but not in a TJ Maxx fall-candle collection kind of way. My mom's side of the family is Lebanese, and when we cook, we incorporate cinnamon into all kinds of savory dishes. (My mom famously makes an incredible cinnamon-rubbed Thanksgiving turkey, but that's another story for another cookbook.) This is one of my favorite examples of using the spice in a subtle but majorly impactful way. Here, stew meat and green beans are infused during the simmering process with a comforting warmth you may not be able to pinpoint in the final dish . . . but it's definitely there and tingles the senses.

1. To a large sauté pan or skillet over medium-high heat, add the oil and heat until shimmering. Add the beef, coriander, and cumin and season with salt and pepper to taste. Cook for 7 to 8 minutes, stirring occasionally, until slightly browned.
2. Add the onion and cook for 5 minutes, until slightly softened. Pour in the beef broth and passata, then add the cinnamon sticks and stir. Bring to a simmer, then reduce the heat to low and cover with a lid or aluminum foil. Let simmer, where gentle bubbles break the surface, for at least 1½ hours, checking every half hour. It should have a thick stew consistency, with the meat submerged in the sauce.
3. Add the green beans and simmer, covered, for 20 minutes. For softer green beans, simmer for an extra 10 minutes. Season with more salt and pepper to taste and serve with the warm pita.

amp it up

I love to dig into this with just some pita, but our Lebanese family always has buttery vermicelli rice on hand, and it's so easy to make for this dish. Just sauté a big handful of broken angel hair pasta or vermicelli noodles in 4 tablespoons butter until golden brown, then add one cup of well-rinsed long-grain white rice and 2 cups water. Reduce the heat to low, cover with a lid, and cook for 20 minutes.

Don't
mess with
Texas
NELSON
33
ROYITO'S
ALL NATURAL
ALL FRESH
HOT SAUCE
ROYITO'S
ALL NATURAL
ALL FRESH
HOT SAUCE

6 ingredients

one dish

royito's carne guisada

My grandfather on my dad's side grew up in the Texas border town of Eagle Pass, and he spoke Spanish before English. His name was Roy, and he named my dad Roy, so to all my dad's childhood friends, he was known as Royito ("Little Roy" in Spanish), a name that's followed him throughout his life. Dad has an absolutely addictive secret salsa recipe that all our family and friends call "Royito's," and we pretty much put it on everything. While Dad still won't even give me, his only son, the exact measurements for his recipe, I've watched him make it enough that I am able to whip up Royito's (Shay's Version) when the mood strikes. It's as epic on top of breakfast tacos (see page 36) as it is in cooked dishes, like this Carne Guisada. The salsa cooks down into a thick tomato gravy that gives a glistening coat to the tender beef. Serve it with rice and beans or just warm flour tortillas for a perfect one-pan (plus a blender) comfort meal.

prep time
10 minutes

cook time
3 hours

yield
serves 4–6

- 2lb (900g) beef stew meat
- 2 tsp kosher salt, plus more to taste
- 1 tsp freshly ground black pepper
- 7 plum tomatoes (about 2lb), divided
- 3 small serrano peppers, divided
- 1 medium red onion, divided
- Juice of 1 lemon, divided
- Warm flour tortillas, to serve

1. Preheat the oven to 325°F (160°C).
2. In a large casserole dish, add the beef in an even layer and season with 2 teaspoons of the salt and the pepper. Set aside.
3. In a blender, add 6 of the tomatoes, 2 of the serranos, ¾ of the onion, half of the lemon juice, 2 cups of water, and a pinch of salt. Blend until smooth. Pour over the beef in the casserole dish. Cover with a lid or aluminum foil and bake for 2 hours.
4. To make the pico de gallo, chop the remaining tomato, onion, and serrano (seeds removed). Transfer to a small bowl with the remaining lemon juice. Season with salt and pepper to taste and set aside.
5. Turn the oven up to 400°F (200°C), remove the lid from the casserole dish, and cook for another hour so the liquid can reduce and the beef can slightly brown on top, until fork tender. Remove from the oven and stir in the pico de gallo. Serve with warm tortillas on the side.

why not sear?

For braises like this, I was always taught to sear the meat first before adding the liquid since the caramelization adds extra flavor . . . but I don't bother with that anymore. Instead, I add the raw meat directly to the braising liquid, let it cook with the lid on until tender, then remove the lid for the end of the cooking process. The oven will actually caramelize the sauce around the meat, and you've saved yourself time and potential oil splatter.

seafood & vegetarian

6 ingredients
no chop
one dish

buttery roasted cod
with garlic-and-herb tomatoes

prep time
10 minutes

cook time
35 minutes

yield
serves 4

12oz (340g) tomatoes, preferably on the vine
1½ cups white wine
¼ cup olive oil
8 garlic cloves, peeled and crushed
6 thyme sprigs
Kosher salt and freshly ground black pepper, to taste
2 tsp za'atar
1½lb (680g) cod fillets or any mild white fish
4 tbsp salted butter
Crusty bread, to serve

While a mild white fish like cod is generally one of the more forgiving proteins, its low-fat content does make it prone to drying and overcooking. That's why I have a few insurance policies. For this recipe, we are cooking at a lower temperature in a garlicky wine jacuzzi, covered for most of the cooking process so the whole dish retains moisture. Adding olive oil and a pat of butter on each fillet also provides enough fat and flavor to ensure a rich and juicy final dish. You'll know it's done when the fish effortlessly flakes with a fork and the tomatoes start to soften and burst. Serve with crusty bread, because this is another dippin' dinner.

1. Preheat the oven to 325°F (160°C).
2. To a 9 x 9-inch (23 x 23cm) baking dish or large, oven-safe skillet, add the tomatoes, wine, olive oil, garlic, and thyme and season with salt and pepper to taste.
3. Season the cod with the za'atar plus more salt and pepper to taste and nestle the fillets between the tomatoes. Top each fillet with a tablespoon of butter, cover with aluminum foil, and bake for 25 minutes.
4. Remove the foil and bake for another 10 minutes, until the cod is tender and flaky. Serve with the crusty bread for dipping.

frozen is fine

Living on an island, I'll often make this dish with locally caught fresh fish like mahi mahi or tilefish, but if I'm using anything caught elsewhere (like cod), I usually go with frozen fillets and let them thaw in the refrigerator before cooking. Not only is it more economical, but the cod is frozen at peak freshness, and any "fresh" fish you buy at the grocery store has almost certainly been previously frozen anyway, so thawing them yourself will usually result in a fresher fish.

use it up!

If you have leftover thyme, use it in my Cheesy Butternut Squash Pasta Bake (page 113). It's also great in tomato sauces, so you can add a couple of tablespoons to the tomato sauce in my Baked Brie Ratatouille (page 198) or my Burst Tomato-Basil Tortellini (page 94).

30ish minutes

one dish

thai basil red curry
with snapper

There's one foolproof way I like to cook any mild whitefish, whether it's halibut, cod, or in this case, snapper. Season the fillet, make a delicious sauce, then gently poach until flaky. Going this route means you don't have to worry about the fish breaking, like it does when you're searing or grilling. This Thai-inspired version uses a red curry paste, which infuses the fish with fragrant chili, garlic, and lemongrass. Make it a complete meal by serving the snapper with rice. (I use a bag from the freezer aisle, which you can throw in the microwave without having to dirty another pan.)

prep time
10 minutes

cook time
20 minutes

yield
serves 4

Four 6oz (170g) skinless snapper fillets
Kosher salt, to taste
⅓ cup Thai red curry paste
13½oz (400ml) can full-fat coconut milk
1 tbsp fish sauce
1 tsp dark brown sugar
½ cup store-bought matchstick carrots or 1 large carrot, grated
1 red, orange, or yellow bell pepper, sliced
⅓ cup torn basil leaves, preferably Thai basil
2 tbsp fresh lime juice
Cooked rice, to serve
Lime wedges, to serve

1. Season the fish lightly with salt to taste and set aside while you prepare the sauce.
2. In a large skillet or sauté pan over medium heat, add the curry paste and cook for 2 minutes, stirring frequently, until darker and fragrant.
3. Add ½ cup water, the coconut milk, fish sauce, brown sugar, carrots, bell pepper, basil, lime juice, and a pinch of salt. Bring to a simmer and cook for 2 minutes.
4. Reduce the heat to low and add the snapper. Cover with a lid and let cook for 10 minutes, until the fish flakes easily but is still firm. Season with more salt to taste and serve with the rice and lime wedges.

ingredient intel

Fish sauce is made from fermented fish, often anchovies, and is a common background flavor in many Thai dishes, most notably pad Thai. In a small amount, it doesn't add a "fishy" flavor, just some extra saltiness, umami, and intrigue. Since this is the only recipe in the cookbook that calls for fish sauce, though, I don't want you to buy it and never use it again! I recommend using it in place of Worcestershire sauce (which also has fermented anchovies, by the way) in my Caesar dressing (page 82), and it's great to add a dash in stir fries, sauces, and marinades across all types of cuisines.

30ish minutes

one dish

fiery crab fried rice

prep time
15 minutes

cook time
10 minutes

yield
serves 4

3 tbsp soy sauce
2 tbsp sriracha or sambal oelek, plus more to serve
2 tsp light or dark brown sugar
Zest and juice of 1 lime, plus wedges to serve
2 tbsp neutral oil
1 bunch of scallions, sliced, green and white parts separated
4 garlic cloves, grated or minced
1in (2.5cm) piece of ginger, peeled and finely chopped, or ½ tsp ground ginger
2 Fresno peppers, finely chopped
4 cups cooked rice (I use leftover takeout rice or thawed frozen rice)
8oz (225g) lump crab meat, picked over for shells (see note on page 183)

My husband, James, and I have a weekly tradition of "Wednesday Fried Rice." You see, Thursday is trash day in our neighborhood, so Wednesday is the day of the week when I clean out the refrigerator to make sure there's nothing that's gone bad—or may be on the brink but is still salvageable. Whatever falls into the latter category goes into Wednesday Fried Rice. I either use leftover rice from takeout or a bag of store-bought frozen rice that I've thawed.

You can make this on any day, of course, because it's totally customizable. Start by sautéing aromatics, add chilled leftover rice, then bring it all back to life in a sauce made of pantry staples. I'll usually add an egg at the end for my protein component, along with some chopped kimchi, but in this version, I gussy it up with some jumbo lump crab meat, because crab fried rice is my absolute favorite and I want to put my best foot forward for y'all.

1. In a small bowl, whisk together the soy sauce, sriracha, brown sugar, and lime zest and juice. Set aside.
2. In a large nonstick skillet over medium-high heat, add the oil, scallion whites, garlic, ginger, and Fresno peppers. Heat for 1 minute, until sizzling and fragrant. Add the rice and stir until warmed through.
3. Reduce the heat to medium-low and add the spicy soy mixture, then stir constantly for 2 minutes. Add the crab and gently stir to warm through. Finish with a drizzle of sriracha and serve with the lime wedges on the side.

don't mess it up!

Fried rice is one of those dishes where the prep takes longer than the cook, and it's crucial you have everything chopped and ready to go at the stovetop before you get started. If you're scrambling around looking for the rice or trying to mix up the sauce while the aromatics are toasting, that garlic is already burned.

ingredient intel

Fresno peppers are one of my favorite little gems in the produce section—they are small red chilis that are sweeter than a jalapeño and usually a bit less spicy, but they still pack a punch. These peppers are perfect when you don't want that grassier flavor you get with a jalapeño, which can be overpowering.

shell out

After you buy crab meat, it is crucial to transfer it to a bowl and run your hands through it to make sure there are no stray pieces of shell in there—I used to think this was a skippable step until my husband nearly chipped his tooth on something way too crunchy in a crab pasta I made. It's more common than you'd think!

shortcut shrimp scampi risotto

While traditional risotto is made by tediously ladling in hot stock until the rice is cooked, I've learned you can add all the stock at once, straight out of the box, no pre-heating necessary. (Between this and my stance on starting pasta in cold water, I may become public enemy number one to every nonna out there, but that's a risk I'm willing to take in order to save you time and an extra dirty pot.) As long as you stir very frequently (that's one step you can't skip), the starches will release from the rice, and you'll still get that creamy texture without any cream. You will be adding a lot of butter though; that's another nonnegotiable.

prep time
10 minutes

cook time
30 minutes

yield
serves 4

- 8oz (225g) medium shrimp, about 14, peeled and deveined
- ½ tsp kosher salt, plus more to taste
- 4 tbsp butter, softened and divided
- ¼ cup chopped fresh parsley, plus more for garnish
- Zest and juice of 1 lemon
- 2 garlic cloves, grated or minced
- ¼ tsp red pepper flakes (optional)
- 1 cup arborio rice
- ¾ cup white wine
- 4 cups (1 qt) seafood or chicken broth

1. Season the shrimp with the salt and set aside.
2. In a small bowl, mix together 3 tablespoons of the butter with the parsley, lemon zest, garlic, and red pepper flakes, if using. Set aside.
3. In a large pot or skillet over medium heat, melt the remaining 1 tablespoon butter and add the rice; toast for 2 minutes. Add the wine and cook for 3 minutes, stirring frequently until absorbed.
4. Add the broth and increase the heat to high, stirring almost constantly, until boiling, then reduce the heat to medium-low and gently simmer.
5. Cook for 15 minutes, continuing to stir, until most of the broth is absorbed and the rice is creamy but still liquidy.
6. Add the shrimp and cook for another 5 minutes, then finish by stirring in the herb butter and the lemon juice. Season with salt to taste and garnish with more parsley before serving.

don't mess it up!

The easiest way to ruin risotto is to overcook it, and that can happen pretty fast—I would say the first five times I made risotto, it turned into a mushy, gloopy mess. I don't want that for you. Start tasting the rice after about 12 minutes, and then every minute after that. When you feel like it has just a tiny bit of grit left to it (it will be easy to bite into but slightly chalky in the center), go ahead and add the shrimp, because you're at the finish line. By the time the shrimp is cooked, your rice will be perfect . . . so serve it immediately! This is not a make-ahead situation.

30ish minutes

6 ingredients

one dish

orange-miso salmon
with broccolini

prep time
10 minutes

cook time
20 minutes

yield
serves 4

3 tbsp red miso paste
2 tsp honey
2 tsp soy sauce
Zest and juice of 1 orange
14oz (400g) broccolini, ends trimmed
2 tbsp olive oil
Kosher salt and freshly ground black pepper, to taste
2lb (900g) salmon fillets

I spent most of my life hating salmon, because most salmon is a total boring bummer. In the words of Tamra Judge on *The Real Housewives of Orange County* season nine reunion, "that's my OPINION!"

As I've grown older and wiser, I've realized that I only felt this way because most people don't go hard enough with salmon. It's a bold fish that can stand up to bold flavors, so let's not hold back here. Red miso paste, which is far more robust than white miso paste, bears a super savory, earthy, umami flavor that only gets more concentrated as it caramelizes on the fish in the oven. Pair this with simple roasted broccolini, and you've got a complete meal in 30 minutes flat.

1. Preheat the oven to 425°F (220°C).
2. In a medium bowl, whisk together the miso paste, honey, soy sauce, and half the orange juice.
3. Line a large sheet pan with foil, add the broccolini, toss with the olive oil, and season with salt and pepper to taste. Add the salmon fillets, season lightly with salt, and brush the tops and sides with the miso mixture.
4. Bake for 16 to 18 minutes, until browned on top. Top with the orange zest and squeeze over the remaining orange juice.

ingredient intel

Miso paste is made from fermented soybeans, and you can usually either buy the red or white version. Red miso paste has a richer flavor due to a longer fermentation time, which makes it perfect for standing up to a more flavorful fish like salmon. It's also saltier than white miso paste, so go easy on salting the fish before you add the sauce.

summer tomato & cheddar tart

I would never ask you to make from-scratch tart dough unless I thought it was really worth it and really easy. As long as you have a food processor, this buttery, cheesy crust comes together in less than a minute and unlike many pie or tart doughs, after this one chills for a bit, it's smooth, pliable, and easy to roll out. Be sure to use freshly grated cheese, as the pre-shredded stuff from the bag has anti-caking agents that can mess with the dough ratio and doesn't melt as evenly into the crust. Also, while this is definitely best using high-quality, in-season summer tomatoes, the roasting process will concentrate the flavor and improve the quality of any kind you can get, year-round.

prep time
10 minutes, plus chilling time

cook time
25 minutes

yield
serves 4

- 1¾ cup flour, plus more for dusting
- 1 cup freshly grated mild cheddar cheese
- 4 tbsp cold salted butter, cubed
- 2 egg yolks
- ½ tsp kosher salt, plus more to taste
- 2 large ripe tomatoes, sliced
- 2 tbsp extra-virgin olive oil, divided
- ½ cup grated pecorino cheese, divided
- Fresh basil leaves, to serve (optional)

1. To a food processor, add the flour, cheddar cheese, butter, egg yolks, and salt. Pulse, streaming in ⅓ cup cold water, until a smooth dough forms, adding more water by the tablespoon if necessary. Transfer the dough to a lightly floured surface and form a 1-inch-thick (2.5cm) disc. Wrap with plastic wrap and place in the refrigerator for 2 hours, or up to one day. Remove from the refrigerator 10 to 15 minutes before you're ready to prepare it.
2. Preheat the oven to 425°F (220°C). Place the tomatoes in an even layer on paper towels and season lightly with salt. Let sit for 10 minutes to draw out the moisture, then pat the tops dry with more paper towels to help prevent the crust from getting soggy.
3. On lightly floured parchment paper, roll out the dough, rotating the paper regularly until the disc is rolled into a circle with a 14-inch (36cm) diameter. Brush the dough with 1 tablespoon of the olive oil, then top with half the pecorino cheese, leaving a 1½-inch border. Arrange the tomatoes in an even layer over top and fold the crust around the tomatoes. Brush the crust and tomatoes with the remaining 1 tablespoon olive oil.
4. Transfer the tart with the parchment paper to a baking sheet. If you want to use a round baking dish as photographed, cut the parchment around the tart before transferring.
5. Bake for 22 to 25 minutes, until golden brown. Let cool for at least 5 minutes, then serve topped with the remaining pecorino cheese and the basil, if using.

mom's mujadara

tabbouleh with
spiced chickpeas

mom's mujadara

prep time
15 minutes

cook time
1½ hours

yield
serves 8

2 cups brown lentils
4 cups (1 qt) vegetable broth
¼ cup olive oil
2 large white or yellow onions, chopped
1 tsp kosher salt, plus more to taste
½ cup long-grain white rice
Freshly ground black pepper, to taste
1 tbsp lemon juice
Pita, to serve

Not to get sappy, but this recipe is probably closest to my heart—and that's not just because my mom cooked the signature Lebanese meal every week for my family when I was growing up. It also perfectly embodies the spirit of this cookbook—and my cooking philosophy in general. Mujadara is the height of simplicity, made with a handful of ingredients. We always ate mujadara with tabbouleh from our favorite local Lebanese restaurant, but that's optional. The pita, however, is very, very necessary. You're going to want to use it to mop up every last bite.

1. In a large pot over high heat, add the lentils, vegetable broth, and 3 cups water. Bring to a boil, then reduce the heat to medium and simmer, stirring occasionally.
2. Meanwhile, in a skillet over medium-high heat, add the oil and onions. Season with the salt and cook for 20 minutes, stirring often, until very dark brown but not burnt, adjusting the heat if it cooks too quickly.
3. To the pot with the simmering lentils, add the onions and the rice. Reduce the heat to medium-low, cover with a lid, and cook for 1 hour, stirring occasionally to prevent sticking, and adding water ¼ cup at a time if it's too dry, until it's the consistency of a thick stew and the onions have basically disappeared into the dish.
4. Add the lemon juice and season with salt and pepper to taste (it's crucial to add enough salt in this for the flavor to pop) before serving with the pita on the side.

don't mess it up!

How you treat the onions makes or breaks this dish. You've got to take them almost to the edge of disaster without quite burning them, so that intense charred flavor permeates everything as it simmers. You also don't want to cook them over lower heat, which will caramelize them instead of char them and make them too sweet.

30ish minutes

one dish

tabbouleh
with spiced chickpeas

Before she passed, my great-aunt Nene blessed us with the handwritten recipe for her famous tabbouleh, a Middle Eastern herb-and-grain salad that she made for all family affairs. My twist spotlights canned chickpeas rather than traditional bulgur, for a faster, heartier version. First cooking the chickpeas in a skillet is a crucial step because it awakens the spices and allows the beans to soak up that bright, lemony dressing. I think Aunt Nene would have approved if she tried it, but she was a very particular (and incredible) woman.

prep time
15 minutes

cook time
5 minutes

yield
serves 6

⅓ cup extra-virgin olive oil
Zest and juice of 2 lemons
1½ tsp kosher salt
1 tsp freshly ground black pepper
Two 15.5oz (439g) cans chickpeas, drained and rinsed
¾ tsp allspice
¾ tsp cayenne pepper
½ tsp cinnamon
2 cups quartered cherry tomatoes (from 1 pint)
1 small bunch of scallions, sliced
1½ cups chopped curly parsley
¾ cup chopped fresh mint

1. In a small measuring cup or bowl, whisk together the olive oil, lemon zest and juice, salt, and black pepper.
2. In a medium skillet over medium heat, add half the dressing along with the chickpeas, allspice, cayenne, and cinnamon. Cook for 3 minutes, until warmed through and the spices are toasted and fragrant. Transfer to a bowl and place in the refrigerator to cool completely. (You can speed this along by placing the bowl in the freezer for a few minutes.)
3. To the bowl of chilled chickpeas, add the tomatoes, scallions, parsley, and mint. Toss with the remaining lemon dressing. Serve immediately or let chill in the refrigerator overnight before serving.

use it up!

If you have leftover mint, make my Lamb Chops with Feta & Mint Orzo Salad (page 171), or use it instead of basil in my Basil Limoncello Spritz cocktails (page 241). You can even make a mint simple syrup by adding equal parts sugar and water to a saucepan with a handful of mint and letting it simmer for 1 to 2 minutes. Let it cool completely, discard the mint, and store it in the refrigerator to add refreshing sweetness to cocktails. (I'm dreaming of mojitos . . .)

weeknight chana masala
with pickled peppers

prep time
10 minutes

cook time
30 minutes

yield
serves 4–6

2 serrano peppers, sliced and divided
1 large red onion, thinly sliced and divided
⅓ cup red wine vinegar
2 tbsp neutral oil
1 tsp ground coriander
1 tsp ground ginger
2 garlic cloves, grated or minced
Two 15oz (425g) cans chickpeas with the liquid
28oz (794g) can crushed tomatoes
2 tsp garam masala
Kosher salt, to taste
⅓ cup heavy cream or coconut milk
Naan and/or rice, to serve

Trying to authentically recreate my favorite Indian dishes is tricky at home, so I usually just order takeout (there is one Indian restaurant on the island, and I call in at least once a week). The complex flavors require a handful of specialty spices, usually toasted and ground by hand, but using that many ingredients and spending that kind of time sort of defeats the premise of this book. That said, one dish I make that hits the spot in a pinch is stewed chickpeas, inspired by my go-to order: chana masala.

Other than a can of beans, the rest of what you'll need should be stocked in your pantry or spice cabinet if it's not already. To achieve a deep flavor quickly, you'll want to bloom the spices in oil first, then finish with a heavy hit of garam masala—a blend that generally contains coriander, cumin, cinnamon, cloves, cardamom, and nutmeg. It's a true powerhouse ingredient that provides so many different rich notes in just a couple teaspoons. Stir in pickled peppers and onions right before serving for a welcome bit of tang and spice, which I like to tame with just a bit of heavy cream—not authentic to chana masala, but pleasing to my personal palate.

1. In a small bowl, add about ¼ of the serrano peppers, ¼ of the onions, and the vinegar to quickly pickle. Set aside.
2. In a large skillet over medium heat, add the oil and the remaining serrano peppers and onions and cook for 5 minutes, until softened. Add the coriander, ginger, and garlic and cook for 1 more minute, until fragrant.
3. Add the chickpeas with the liquid and the tomatoes, increase the heat to high, and bring to a simmer. Lower the heat and simmer, stirring often, for 20 minutes, or until thickened.
4. Stir in the garam masala and salt, to taste, and cook for 1 minute, then stir in the heavy cream. Finish by adding the pickled peppers and onions, along with 1 tablespoon of the pickling liquid. Serve with the naan.

use it up!

If you don't cook many Indian dishes or curries, you might be puzzled about how else to use the garam masala you bought. The savory-sweet spice blend is a great addition to certain soups and stews. You can use it in lieu of the curry powder in my Curry Tomato Soup (page 63) or stir a teaspoon into Mom's Mujadara (page 192), but it also works in desserts—try it out in pumpkin pie instead of the usual pumpkin pie spice . . . Trust me.

30ish minutes

one dish

chili-lime corn & black bean tacos

After years of exploring Disney World as a food writer and content creator, perhaps the most surprising thing I discovered is that there are incredible vegetarian options at every single dining location throughout the park. Some are, of course, better than others, and I'm partial to the options that don't use imitation meat. Over at Animal Kingdom, they used to have a stand that had excellent street corn and black bean tacos, and this recipe brings a little bit of Disney nostalgia back home with me. It couldn't be easier: Just throw everything in a skillet, heat through, and you've got dinner. You can char fresh cobs yourself, but I find that using frozen fire-roasted corn is just as tasty and saves a whole lot of time.

prep time
10 minutes

cook time
10 minutes

yield
serves 4

- 12oz (340g) frozen fire-roasted corn
- 15oz (425g) can black beans, drained and rinsed
- 1 cup quartered cherry or grape tomatoes
- 1 large jalapeño, seeds removed, chopped
- 1 medium shallot, minced
- 1 tbsp ancho chili powder
- 2 garlic cloves, grated or minced
- Zest and juice of 1 lime
- 2 tbsp extra-virgin olive oil
- ½ tsp kosher salt, plus more to taste
- ½ cup crumbled queso fresco
- Warm tortillas, to serve
- Lime wedges, to serve

1. In a large bowl, add the corn, beans, tomatoes, jalapeño, shallot, chili powder, garlic, lime zest and juice, and olive oil. Season with the salt and toss everything to coat.
2. Place a large skillet over medium heat and add the mixture, cooking for 5 minutes, until warmed through.
3. Stir in half the queso fresco, season with more salt to taste, and top with the remaining queso fresco. Serve buffet-style with the tortillas and lime wedges.

make it a cookout

Since this is such a summery recipe, I like to prepare the taco filling in a bowl (following step one), then take it outside and place a cast-iron skillet directly over the grill for step two. You can char the tortillas right alongside the filling, then put the skillet out for your guests to serve themselves.

baked brie ratatouille

prep time
20 minutes

cook time
1¼ hour

yield
serves 4

- 2 cups passata
- 1 medium shallot, thinly sliced
- 3 garlic cloves, grated or minced
- 1½ tsp herbes de Provence, divided
- 1½ tsp kosher salt, divided
- 1 tsp freshly ground black pepper, divided
- 1 medium zucchini, sliced
- 1 small eggplant, sliced
- 3 medium tomatoes, sliced
- 3 tbsp olive oil, divided
- 8oz (225g) wheel of brie
- Sliced baguette, to serve

This is one of those meals that looks really elegant, but all you have to do is assemble everything and let the oven do all the work for you. The tomato sauce at the bottom will concentrate in flavor as it cooks down with all the vegetables, while the buttery brie center complements the natural tartness and sweetness in the dish and will melt into the sauce and vegetables. It works as an easy vegetarian dinner, or as a party snack with baguette slices so everyone can assemble their own little sandwiches.

1. Preheat the oven to 350°F (180°C).
2. In a 12-inch, 3.5-quart (3.3L) round casserole dish or oven-safe skillet, add the passata, shallot, garlic, 1 teaspoon of the herbes de Provence, 1 teaspoon of the salt, and ½ teaspoon of the black pepper. Stir to combine.
3. Starting at the outer edge of the dish, arrange the vegetables in concentric circles, working inward, alternating the vegetables and overlapping the slices so that a little bit of each slice is visible.
4. Drizzle 2 tablespoons of the olive oil over top and sprinkle with the remaining ½ teaspoon herbes de Provence, the remaining ½ teaspoon salt, and the remaining ½ teaspoon pepper. Cover with aluminum foil and bake for 45 minutes, until the vegetables start to soften.
5. Remove the foil and bake for another 15 minutes, then remove the pan from the oven.
6. Nestle the brie into the center and drizzle the remaining tablespoon olive oil over top. Return to the oven and bake for 10 minutes, until the cheese is melted. Serve with the sliced baguette.

ingredient intel

Herbes de Provence is a seasoning blend that gets its name because it's made of dried herbs commonly grown in the Provence region in the south of France, like thyme, rosemary, oregano, savory, marjoram, and sometimes lavender. It actually has similar ingredients to Italian seasoning (see note on page 159), so you can substitute that in a pinch.

party snacks

nacho cheesecake

prep time
10 minutes

cook time
25 minutes

yield
serves 8

1 tbsp neutral oil
1lb (450g) ground beef or turkey
2 tbsp taco seasoning
15oz (425g) can black beans, drained and rinsed
15oz (425g) can diced tomatoes with green chiles with the juices, divided
6oz (170g) sturdy tortilla chips (see note below)
4 cups shredded Mexican cheese blend
8oz (225g) Velveeta cheese, cubed
¼ cup whole milk
Pickled jalapeños and pico de gallo, to serve

If you're already a friend of the show, you know that I'm a connoisseur of what I call "sleazy cheese," more commonly known as nacho cheese. You'd also know that I love chain restaurants and live for a dramatic plate of nachos, so what we have here is a hybrid of two of America's most beloved nacho towers: Guy Fieri's Flavortown trash can nachos and Jimmy Buffett's Margaritaville volcano nachos. My signature technique here is baking them in a springform pan, which facilitates crusty cheesy edges and provides the opportunity for an impressive party trick reveal.

1. Preheat the oven to 375°F (190°C).
2. In a medium skillet over medium-high heat, add the oil and heat until shimmering. Add the beef and seasoning and cook for 8 minutes, until browned and crumbled.
3. Stir in the black beans and half the diced tomatoes. Cook for 2 minutes, until warmed through.
4. In a springform pan, add a layer of chips, then top with the meat mixture and a layer of the shredded cheese. Continue layering, forming a cone-shaped volcano. Top with more shredded cheese and bake for 12 minutes, until melted.
5. Meanwhile, wipe the skillet clean and set it over medium-low heat. Add the Velveeta, milk, and remaining diced tomatoes. Cook for 5 minutes, until melted.
6. Drizzle the sleazy cheese over the nachos and remove the outer ring of the springform pan for a dramatic reveal when serving. Top with the pickled jalapeños and pico de gallo.

don't mess it up!

Nachos of this magnitude require a thick tortilla chip—if you use the thinner, more brittle ones, the nachos will collapse into a soggy mess. My personal favorite brand in this instance is Santitas!

whipped ricotta dip with pistachio-artichoke pesto

chopped italiano sliders

30ish minutes

one dish

whipped ricotta dip

with pistachio-artichoke pesto

prep time
15 minutes

yield
serves 8–10

- 1 cup shelled roasted pistachios
- 1 cup grated Parmesan cheese
- 3 garlic cloves, roughly chopped
- 4 cups arugula
- 12oz (340g) jar artichoke hearts packed in oil, reserve 1 tbsp of the oil
- Zest and juice of 1 lemon
- 1 cup olive oil, plus more to serve
- 1½ tsp kosher salt, plus more to taste
- 32oz (907g) container whole milk ricotta
- Freshly ground black pepper, to taste

Store-bought pesto can be a useful shortcut ingredient when you're using it in the background of a dish for a little flavor boost (see my Laze-agna, page 110). But if pesto is going to be the star of the show, I'll always make my own. It takes just a couple of minutes in a food processor, and there are so many ingredients you can play around with, beyond classic basil. For this bright, lemony artichoke pesto, instead of pine nuts, I use pistachios, which stand up to everything else going on in the mix. Add ricotta cheese, and you've got an impressive, no-cook party dip.

1. In a large food processor, add the pistachios, Parmesan, and garlic and pulse for 1 minute until well combined.
2. Add the arugula, artichoke hearts, marinating oil, lemon zest and juice, olive oil, and salt. Pulse until fully combined, then transfer about ¼ of the pesto to a small bowl and set aside.
3. To the food processor, add the ricotta and pulse until smooth. Season with salt and pepper to taste.
4. Transfer to a serving bowl and top with the reserved pesto and a drizzle of olive oil.

diy appetizer

I love to serve this on a platter with halved, hollowed-out mini sweet peppers and prosciutto. Guests can fill the peppers with the dip and wrap it in prosciutto for the perfect little popper.

use it up!

This makes a lot of dip, so if you have leftovers, it works great as a sandwich spread or tossed with hot pasta.

30ish minutes

one dish

chopped italiano sliders

I'm a lazy but loving entertainer, and this party dish comes together super quick. I like to serve it with slider buns so people can create their own sandwiches or simply eat the components as a salad. The move here is to really finely chop everything so you get all the flavors in one bite. I prefer using soppressata, coppa, and salami, because you get a mix of spices and textures, but any Italian cured meats will do!

prep time
30 minutes

yield
serves 8

¼ cup mayonnaise
¼ cup extra-virgin olive oil
2 tbsp red wine vinegar
2 tsp Italian seasoning
1 tsp kosher salt
1 tsp freshly ground black pepper
1lb (450g) romaine lettuce, finely chopped
4oz (115g) provolone cheese, finely chopped
6oz (170g) cured Italian meats
1 medium red onion, finely chopped
12oz (340g) jar roasted red peppers, finely chopped
¼ cup finely chopped banana peppers
Slider buns

1. In a large bowl, whisk together the mayonnaise, olive oil, vinegar, Italian seasoning, salt, and pepper.
2. Add the romaine lettuce, provolone, cured meats, red onion, roasted red peppers, and banana peppers, and toss to thoroughly combine. Serve it alongside the slider buns.

use it up!

If you have leftover banana peppers, they are also great for adding a tangy spice to homemade pizzas—try them on my Italian Beef and Giardiniera Pan Pizza (page 118).

easy bruschetta

For an extra addition to this spread, simply chop up the best tomatoes you can find, mix them with a handful of torn fresh basil, a big glug of high quality extra-virgin olive oil and season with salt to taste. Sometimes I'll add a splash of balsamic, too, but if the tomatoes are in peak season I don't want it to compete with their natural sweetness and acidity.

30ish minutes

6 ingredients

one dish

garlic-knot pigs in a blanket

If you haven't noticed yet, I'm very into taking two things I love and bringing them together into an even better thing. (Cue "2 Become 1" by the Spice Girls . . . Sorry, I'm starting to age myself with these deep-cut song references that only millennial gay men and women still appreciate.) Consider this recipe another staple for your party snack portfolio as classic pigs in a blanket get brushed with hot garlic butter straight out of the oven.

prep time
10 minutes

cook time
15 minutes

yield
makes 25

- 12oz (340g) package smoked cocktail wieners or franks, such as Lit'l Smokies, patted dry
- 8oz (226g) tube refrigerated crescent rolls, cut into 1in (2.5cm) strips
- 4 tbsp butter, melted and divided
- 2 garlic cloves, grated or minced
- ¼ cup grated Parmesan cheese
- 2 tbsp chopped fresh parsley
- Marinara sauce, to serve

1. Preheat the oven to 375°F (190°C).
2. Wrap the cocktail wieners in strips of dough and press to seal. Place on a sheet pan about 1 inch (2.5cm) apart, brush with 1 tablespoon of the butter and bake for 12 to 15 minutes, or until nicely browned.
3. Add the garlic to the remaining melted butter. When the knots come out of the oven, brush with the garlic butter and sprinkle with Parmesan and parsley. Serve with the marinara.

swap it out

I like to use crescent-roll dough when I feel like having that buttery, flaky flavor of a traditional pig in a blanket, but this is also great using strips of pizza dough, which makes for a fluffier crust that's perfect if you really want to lean into the garlic-knot vibe.

use it up!

If you have leftover parsley (and you will, since you're only using a bit here), try my Tabbouleh with Spiced Chickpeas (page 193)—it works great as a salad green all on its own! You can also use it to make the chimichurri I put on my cheesy Honeymoon Choripán (page 89) or my Green Godd-ish dressing (page 73).

30ish minutes

6 ingredients

one dish

sizzling garlic shrimp a la schiller's

prep time
10 minutes

cook time
10 minutes

yield
serves 6–8

If I ever had my own Cheers, it was Schiller's Liquor Bar, a boisterous yet refined French brasserie in New York City's Lower East Side that closed in 2017. During our early days of dating, James and I spent too many nights there, sipping Manhattans over a cast-iron skillet of their garlic shrimp, which came out still sizzling like a platter of Chili's fajitas. I've since tried to reverse engineer that experience from memory. The secret is using a mix of butter and olive oil, and you don't add the garlic until the last 15 to 30 seconds of cooking, because you want it to mellow out slightly but still pack a punch.

¼ cup olive oil
2lb (900g) medium shrimp, peeled and deveined, tails removed
Kosher salt, to taste
4 tbsp butter, cut into small pieces
8 garlic cloves, peeled and sliced (I always buy pre-peeled cloves for this)
¼ cup chopped fresh parsley
1 tsp red pepper flakes
1 tbsp lemon juice
Crusty bread, to serve

1. In a large skillet over medium-low heat, add the olive oil and slowly heat for 5 minutes. Season the shrimp with salt to taste and add to the skillet, quickly cooking for 2 minutes per side.
2. Increase the heat to medium-high and add the butter and garlic. Cook for another 30 seconds, until sizzling. Remove from the heat.
3. Stir in the parsley, red pepper flakes, and lemon juice. Serve immediately with the crusty bread for dipping.

don't mess it up!

Similar to my French Onion Steak Bites (page 168), the garlic here is going into a very hot pan, which means it will burn very quickly, so you really have to turn off the heat and get it away from the hot burner almost immediately after you add it. It should turn a very light golden color, but any darker than that and you'll get an acrid flavor.

30ish minutes

no chop

party shrimp
with champagne cocktail sauce

I first came up with this recipe because I just liked the play on words of "champagne cocktail sauce," but after tinkering around to find the right ratios, I actually prefer this to classic cocktail sauce, which relies on lemon juice for its acidity. Champagne vinegar has a mild, fruity tartness that serves as a solid background for the zip of the horseradish, while crème fraîche tames everything and adds an extra little hit of tang. I use Ina Garten's method of roasting the shrimp because it yields the perfect texture every time, but for a shortcut, feel free to buy pre-cooked shrimp from the store. Then all you have to do is stir the sauce together and get the party started.

prep time
5 minutes

cook time
10 minutes

yield
serves 4–6

2lb (900g) shrimp, peeled and deveined (I buy pre-peeled shrimp)
2 tbsp olive oil
Kosher salt and freshly ground black pepper, to taste
¾ cup ketchup
⅓ cup crème fraîche
2 tbsp champagne vinegar
1½ tbsp prepared horseradish
2 tsp Worcestershire sauce
1 tsp lemon juice

1. Preheat the oven to 400°F (200°C).
2. On a large sheet pan, place the shrimp in an even layer, coat with the olive oil, and season with salt and pepper to taste. Roast for 10 minutes, until pink and firm. Remove from the oven and let cool or transfer to the refrigerator to chill completely.
3. Meanwhile, in a small bowl, mix together the ketchup, crème fraîche, champagne vinegar, horseradish, Worcestershire sauce, and lemon juice. Serve with the chilled shrimp.

ingredient intel

Crème fraîche may have gained notoriety as a pretentious ingredient peddled by chefs in a certain South Park episode, but it really is awesome—it's basically a French version of sour cream that's richer, smoother, and a little less tangy. I love it because it's great in both raw preparations like this sauce but also can stand up to higher heat without curdling the way sour cream can, which is why I also use it in my Jalapeño Popper Hot Crab Dip (page 219).

30ish minutes

no chop

one dish

cubano dogs

prep time
10 minutes

cook time
15 minutes

yield
makes 8 sandwiches

8 hot dogs
8 split-top hot dog buns
3 tbsp butter, melted
1 tsp garlic powder
½ tsp ground cumin
½ tsp dried oregano
16 slices of Swiss cheese
8 thin slices of deli ham
8 pickle spears, to serve
Yellow mustard, to serve

Another local delicacy in Key West is the Cubano—a pressed sandwich, filled with ham, mojo, Swiss cheese, roast pork, pickles, and mustard. We could argue all day over who has the best one; all I know is I'm not competing with any of them. I'm much more comfortable in the hot dog space, so this recipe highlights the same savory, tangy flavors but with a frank in place of the slow-braised pork. Split the dogs down the center to maximize the searing surface area. The pickle spear fits in perfectly at the end, too, which is quite satisfying.

1. Preheat the oven to 425°F (220°C).
2. Slice the hot dogs lengthwise without cutting all the way through them. Spread them open slightly and place them on a small sheet pan. Bake for 5 minutes.
3. Meanwhile, stir the melted butter with the garlic powder, cumin, and oregano and brush the buns inside and out with the spiced butter. Line each bun with 2 pieces of cheese and 1 piece of ham.
4. Remove the hot dogs from the oven and place one inside each bun. Return to the oven for 2 to 3 minutes, or until the cheese is melted. Serve with a pickle spear nestled into the hot dogs and a drizzle of mustard.

don't mess it up!

When I had friends cross test this recipe, the only real issue that came up was buying slices of ham that were too thick. It's best if you go to the deli counter and ask them to slice it very thinly so it properly lines the bun and doesn't overpower the hot dog.

sweet-heat
island dogs
cubano dogs

30ish minutes

one dish

sweet-heat island dogs

prep time
5 minutes

cook time
10 minutes

yield
makes 8 sandwiches

8oz (225g) mango, finely diced
1 habanero pepper, minced
1 shallot, minced
¼ cup chopped cilantro
Juice of 1 lime
Kosher salt and freshly ground black pepper, to taste
8 hot dogs
8 brioche split-top buns
4 tbsp salted butter, melted
Thai sweet chili sauce, to serve

When you come visit me in Key West, one of our first stops will be Island Dogs, which serves a signature hot dog topped with a tropical fruit salsa on an ultra-buttery toasted bun drizzled with sweet chili sauce. Until then, here's a version you can recreate at home!

1. Preheat the oven to 375°F (190°C).
2. In a medium bowl, stir together the mango, habanero pepper, shallot, cilantro, and lime juice. Season with salt and pepper to taste and set aside.
3. On a large baking sheet, arrange the hot dogs and buns side by side and brush everything with the butter. Bake for 8 minutes, until the hot dogs are warmed through and the buns are toasted.
4. Add a hot dog to each bun and top with the mango salsa. Finish by drizzling each hot dog with the Thai sweet chili sauce.

turn down the heat

The habanero pepper may pack a lot of spice, but it's tamed by the sweetness of the mango in this salsa. However, for a milder alternative, try swapping in a fruity Fresno pepper instead (see note on page 182).

30ish minutes

6 ingredients

one dish

pimento cheese blt dogs

Pimento cheese is a delicacy I learned about later in life, and I love it as a simple dip. (One of my favorite unlikely combinations is pairing it with salt-and-vinegar potato chips . . . Not going to tell you my mental state when I discovered that, though.) It's also amazing on a BLT, and in this case, a BLT hot dog. My favorite store-bought version is called MyThreeSons because it has the perfect amount of mayo to hold everything together without being too gloopy.

prep time
10 minutes

cook time
15 minutes

yield
makes 8 sandwiches

Cooking spray or oil
8 jumbo beef franks (see note below)
8 slices of thin center-cut bacon
8 split-top hot dog buns
10oz (285g) pimento cheese
1 cup shredded iceberg lettuce
½ cup chopped tomatoes

1. Preheat the oven to 400° (200°C). Line a small sheet pan with foil and grease with the cooking spray.
2. Wrap each hot dog in a slice of bacon and transfer to the lined sheet pan. Bake for 12 to 15 minutes, until the bacon is crispy. Alternatively, you can grill these over medium heat, turning frequently until the bacon is crispy.
3. Spread each bun with the pimento cheese and arrange them on a platter. Add a hot dog to each bun and top with the lettuce and tomatoes.

don't mess it up!

The only problem with bacon-wrapped dogs is that oftentimes the hot dogs get overcooked and shriveled before the bacon can fully crisp. That's why I always go for very thin slices of bacon (center cut is leaner and therefore crisps faster), and a plumper hot dog (Hebrew National jumbo beef franks are a personal favorite).

jalapeño popper hot crab dip

I believe it's very important to have at least two or three interesting party dips in your repertoire, because the crowd goes wild for dips. You can show up and be like, "This is my signature dip," and everyone will associate you with an addictive creation and talk about it for years. It's an emotional connection that I've found only really applies to dips. This is one of my go-tos because it requires very little prep and comes together in one big skillet. And now it can be yours, too.

prep time
15 minutes

cook time
35 minutes

yield
serves 6

- 5 slices of center-cut bacon, chopped
- 8oz (225g) lump crab meat, picked over for shells (see note on page 183)
- 2 tsp Old Bay seasoning
- 1 tsp garlic powder
- 12oz (340g) whipped cream cheese
- ½ cup crème fraîche
- ½ cup shredded mild cheddar cheese
- ⅓ cup chopped fresh parsley, plus more to serve
- ¼ cup chopped pickled jalapeños, plus 1 tbsp of the brine
- Saltine crackers, to serve

1. Preheat the oven to 350°F (180°C).
2. In a large oven-safe skillet over medium heat, add the bacon and cook for 6 minutes, until crispy.
3. Add the crab meat and toss to coat in the bacon fat for 2 minutes, then season with the Old Bay and garlic powder.
4. Remove from the heat and stir in the cream cheese, crème fraîche, cheddar, parsley, and pickled jalapeños and brine. Flatten into an even layer with the back of a spoon.
5. Bake for 25 minutes, or until hot and bubbly. Serve in the skillet with the crackers on the side.

30ish minutes

one dish

nashville hot chicken & pickle dip

prep time
20 minutes

cook time
5 minutes

yield
serves 6–8

I first saw the viral "fried pickle dip" on Instagram from @mad_about_food in 2024. My version gives you the same flavors and textures without any frying involved. You chop pickles, swirl them into a cool and creamy dip, and top with crunchy, toasted Japanese panko breadcrumbs. I go a step further, drawing inspiration from Nashville hot chicken spices that are incorporated into the dip and the breadcrumb topping. One bite takes me back to Prince's Hot Chicken in Nashville, one of my favorite restaurants in the world.

- 4 cups shredded rotisserie chicken
- 12oz (340g) whipped cream cheese
- 8oz (225g) sour cream
- ½ cup cayenne-pepper hot sauce, such as Texas Pete or Crystal
- ½ cup chopped dill pickles and 2 tbsp of the brine, plus more pickles to serve
- Kosher salt, to taste
- 3 tbsp salted butter
- 1 tsp cayenne
- 1 tsp garlic powder
- 1 tsp onion powder
- ½ cup panko breadcrumbs
- Fresh dill, for garnish (optional)
- Crinkle-cut potato chips, to serve

1. In a large bowl, add the chicken, cream cheese, sour cream, hot sauce, pickles and brine, and salt; stir until combined.
2. In a small skillet over medium heat, add the butter, cayenne, garlic powder, and onion powder and heat until the butter is melted. Add the panko and cook, stirring frequently for 3 minutes, or until nicely browned.
3. Plate the dip, top with the toasted breadcrumbs, and sprinkle with more pickles and garnish with fresh dill, if desired. Serve with the chips.

make it ahead

If you're having a party and want to prep something ahead, this is the perfect dish for that. You can make the dip up to 2 days ahead and cover it tightly with plastic wrap in the refrigerator, and the breadcrumbs can be made the day before and stored in an airtight container at room temperature. When it's time to serve, simply add the breadcrumbs on top and garnish with the extra pickles.

Joe

baked feta, spinach & artichoke dip

Remember that baked feta tomato pasta from TikTok? Of course you do; we all have collective trauma from watching that block of cheese hit the center of a casserole dish ten thousand times in a row. That being said, I did try out the dish and have to admit . . . it's pretty damn good. This one's a riff, in the form of spinach-artichoke dip, which in my opinion is far and away a superior method. Because eating a whole block of feta as a pasta meal is insane, but as a dip, it's socially acceptable. Plus, I just prefer the chunkier texture of the feta this way rather than in a sauce. So many recipes overcomplicate spinach dip, and I hate using frozen spinach, waiting for it to thaw, then having to squeeze the dickens out of it to remove all the water. Fresh greens wilt right in the melty cheese, and it tastes even better.

prep time
10 minutes

cook time
35 minutes

yield
serves 4–6

8oz (225g) feta cheese, crumbled
16oz (450g) cream cheese, cut into bite-size pieces
2 cups quartered cherry tomatoes (from 1 pint)
12oz (340g) jar marinated artichoke hearts, plus 2 tbsp of the marinating oil
3 garlic cloves, grated or minced
2 tsp dried oregano or za'atar
½ tsp red pepper flakes
5oz (140g) fresh spinach, roughly chopped
1 cup grated Asiago or Parmesan cheese
1 cup shredded mozzarella cheese
Pita chips, to serve
Veggies, to serve

1 Preheat the oven to 375°F (190°C).

2 In a 4-quart (3.7L) casserole dish, add the feta, cream cheese, tomatoes, artichoke hearts and marinating oil, garlic, oregano, and red pepper flakes. Stir to combine. Cover with foil and bake for 20 minutes.

3 Remove the casserole dish from the oven. Add the spinach and stir until combined. Top with the Asiago and mozzarella and bake, uncovered, for another 12 to 15 minutes, until brown and bubbly. Serve with the pita chips and veggies for dipping.

ingredient intel

Jarred or canned artichokes generally come packed in either water or oil, similar to the marinated cheeses I use in other recipes in this book (like my Lamb Chops with Feta & Mint Orzo Salad, page 171). In this dip, the oil-packed artichokes come with flavor enhancers like garlic and herbs that instantly add more bang for your buck.

loaded steak & queso fries

prep time
10 minutes

cook time
20 minutes

yield
serves 4

Whenever I visit Southern California, I am medically required to go to any local Mexican spot for carne asada–loaded fries (think crispy potatoes piled high with nacho fixings). This sheet-pan version was inspired by those wonderful experiences, adjusted with some shortcuts. While most traditional carne asada is marinated in vinegar and citrus juices to tenderize the beef before it's charred, I wanted to make a fast and loose rendition with simpler seasoning. Skirt steak is a perfect cut because it doesn't need tenderization if you thinly slice it against the grain. Lay it on a bed of garlicky crinkle fries and smother with this three-ingredient queso that has a pleasing bite from the pepper jack cheese.

32oz (907g) bag frozen crinkle-cut fries
2 tsp neutral oil
12oz (340g) skirt steak
Kosher salt and freshly ground black pepper, to taste
2 tsp garlic powder, divided
2 tsp ancho chili powder
1 tsp ground cumin
1 tsp onion powder
12oz (354ml) can evaporated milk
4oz (115g) white Velveeta cheese
6oz (170g) pepper jack cheese, grated
Your favorite toppings, such as pico de gallo and guacamole, to serve

1. Prepare the frozen fries according to package instructions.
2. Meanwhile, in a medium skillet over high heat, add the oil until shimmering but not smoking. Season the steak with salt and pepper to taste, 1 teaspoon of the garlic powder, and the chili powder, cumin, and onion powder. Sear for 3 to 4 minutes per side, until nicely browned, then transfer to a cutting board to rest for 10 minutes before thinly slicing against the grain. Set aside.
3. In a small saucepan over medium heat, add the evaporated milk and Velveeta, stirring frequently until melted. Turn the heat to low and stir in the pepper jack, one handful at a time, until melted. (You can keep this warm on very low heat, stirring occasionally, until you're ready to assemble.)
4. On a serving platter (or the sheet pan you cooked them on), toss the hot fries with the remaining 1 teaspoon garlic powder. Top with the sliced steak and drizzle with the queso and desired toppings. Serve immediately.

don't mess it up!

I like how the fries get a little soggy from the queso; it's part of the experience. But if you want them to stand their ground better, cook for a couple of minutes longer than advised on the package directions, so they stay extra crispy.

bust a myth

Common wisdom has always been to let your steak come to room temperature because the beef will cook more evenly this way. Serious Eats food scientist J. Kenji López-Alt conducted an experiment and found that a steak rested for two hours at room temperature yielded no difference from a steak straight out of the refrigerator. So no need to waste your time!

cheeseburger wontons

The cheeseburger spring rolls from the snack cart at the entrance of Adventureland in the Magic Kingdom are a cult favorite among Disney adults, and this is my tribute to them. Rather than fussing with rolling or frying, whip out your trusty mini muffin tin, line the cups with wonton wrappers, parbake them, add a savory beef filling, and finish in the oven for a few more minutes. This method is also great for homemade crab rangoons, if you're into that sort of thing.

prep time
10 minutes

cook time
25 minutes

yield
makes 24 wontons

- Cooking spray
- 24 wonton wrappers
- 1lb (450g) ground beef
- 1 tsp garlic powder
- 1 tsp paprika
- 1 tsp kosher salt
- 1 tsp freshly ground black pepper
- 2 tbsp yellow mustard
- 1 tbsp Worcestershire sauce
- 1 medium onion, finely diced, divided
- ¼ cup pickle relish, plus more to serve
- 5 slices of American cheese, torn into small pieces
- 1 cup burger sauce, preferably Sir Kensington's Special Sauce, to serve

1. Preheat the oven to 350°F (180°C).
2. Coat a 24-cup mini muffin tin with cooking spray and line each cup with a wonton wrapper. Spray the wrappers with more cooking spray. Bake for 8 minutes, until slightly crispy.
3. Meanwhile, in a large nonstick skillet over medium heat, add the beef, garlic powder, paprika, salt, and pepper. Cook for 8 minutes, until brown and crumbled.
4. Add the mustard, Worcestershire sauce, half the onion, and the relish. Cook for another 2 minutes. Add the American cheese and ⅓ cup water and cook, stirring, for 5 minutes, until the cheese is melted.
5. Fill each wonton cup with a heaping tablespoon of the filling and return to the oven for another 10 minutes. Remove from the oven and let cool for at least 5 minutes. Garnish with more relish and the remaining onion and serve with the burger sauce.

don't mess it up!

Depending on your oven, the edges of the wontons may start to get too dark before the bottom and sides get crisp. If you notice this happening, remove the pan from the oven and loosely (and carefully) cover the whole pan with aluminum foil, then continue baking.

desserts & cocktails

no chop

one dish

mixed-berry cardamom cobbler

prep time
10 minutes

cook time
45 minutes

yield
serves 8

4 tbsp salted butter
2 cups self-rising flour
2 tsp ground cardamom
1½ cups plus 1 tbsp sugar, divided
2 cups buttermilk
2 tsp vanilla extract
3 cups mixed berries, fresh or frozen
Vanilla ice cream, to serve

I wish I'd known earlier how incredible cardamom is in desserts. It has a unique floral, citrusy character that can't be replicated or swapped with anything else, which is why it should absolutely be a staple in your spice drawer. I love to put it in coffee cakes, mulled wine during the holidays, or even savory dishes like a coconut curry. Cardamom is particularly appealing in my basic cobbler batter, amplifying the taste of the berries while adding a bit of interest to the sweetness. Choose whichever fruit is calling you—I go for a blend of blackberries, blueberries, and raspberries. And be sure to buy ground cardamom instead of the whole pods for this dish!

1. Preheat the oven to 350°F (180°C).
2. In a 9 x 13-inch (22 x 33cm) baking dish, add the butter and place it in the preheating oven for 8 minutes, until it's melted.
3. Meanwhile, in a large bowl, whisk together the self-rising flour, cardamom, and 1 cup of the sugar. Add the buttermilk and vanilla and whisk until thoroughly combined, then pour into the preheated baking dish with the melted butter.
4. Scatter the berries evenly on top of the batter, sprinkle with the remaining tablespoon of sugar, and bake for 40 to 45 minutes, until deep golden brown on top. Serve hot with the vanilla ice cream.

ingredient intel

Self-rising flour is basically just all-purpose flour that already has a leavening agent (baking powder) in it, so it creates a very fluffy, almost cake-like texture in this cobbler that I love. It's also a great shortcut ingredient for fluffy biscuits—try my recipe on *page 50!*

pecan pie baklawa

not judy's fudge pie

pecan pie baklawa

prep time
15 minutes, plus cooling time

cook time
45 minutes

yield
serves 8

- 4 cups finely chopped pecans, plus more to serve
- 1½ cups light brown sugar, divided
- 1 tsp ground cinnamon
- ½ tsp kosher salt
- Two 16oz (545g) packages phyllo dough, thawed
- 10 tbsp salted butter, melted
- Zest and juice of 1 orange

If there's any dish that represents the ultimate mash-up of my Lebanese and Texas heritage, it's Pecan Pie Baklawa. Traditional Lebanese baklawa is very similar to Greek baklava but typically features walnuts instead of pistachios and is glazed with a simple syrup spiked with orange blossom water—a somewhat tough-to-find ingredient in the US.

Pecan pie always reminds me of my grandfather (Poppy), who had his own pecan trees in his yard in Brownwood, Texas. This dessert has a cinnamon-and-brown-sugar filling like the pies I grew up with, while the orange simple syrup (an imperfect but still absolutely delicious substitute for orange blossom water) brightens everything with a distinct citrus flavor.

1. Preheat the oven to 350°F (180°C). Grease a 9 x 13-inch (22 x 33cm) baking dish.
2. Place the pecans on a sheet pan and toast in the oven for 5 minutes, until fragrant.
3. In a large bowl, add the toasted pecans, 1 cup of the brown sugar, the cinnamon, salt, and ¼ cup water. Use your hands to thoroughly combine.
4. To the prepared baking dish, add 10 sheets of the phyllo dough, brushing between each layer with butter. Top with half of the pecan mixture, then add 5 more sheets of dough, again brushing with butter between each layer, then top with the remaining filling. Finish with 10 more phyllo sheets, brushing with butter between each layer and on top.
5. Use a sharp knife to carefully slice four even rows lengthwise, then 8 rows diagonally to create a diamond shape. Bake for 40 minutes, or until a deep golden brown on top.
6. Meanwhile, in a small saucepan over medium heat, add the remaining ½ cup brown sugar, 1 cup water, plus the orange zest and juice. Let simmer for 5 minutes, then remove from the heat and let cool completely.
7. Spoon the cooled syrup on the hot baklawa when it comes out of the oven and garnish with more chopped pecans on top. Let sit for at least 2 hours at room temperature before serving.

use it up!

If you have leftover phyllo dough, there are so many different uses for it. I've added it on top of chicken pot pie for a more delicate and delightfully crisp alternative to pie crust. It is also great swapped in for the wonton wrappers in my Cheeseburger Wontons (page 227)!

not judy's fudge pie

Judy is one of the most special people in my life, and probably the reason I exist in this world. She's my mom's cousin and my dad's decades-long business partner, and she's the one who introduced my parents to each other. Even though she made her signature fudge pie for everyone in our family each holiday season, she never let us call it "Judy's fudge pie" because she got the recipe from her college roommate and didn't want to take the credit. "Judy's College Roommate's Fudge Pie" doesn't have much of a ring to it, so it will always be Judy's fudge pie to me.

prep time
10 minutes, plus cooling time

cook time
45 minutes

yield
serves 8

- 1 cup salted butter, cut into pieces
- 4oz (113g) bar unsweetened chocolate, preferably the Baker's brand, broken into pieces
- 4 eggs
- 2 cups granulated sugar
- ½ cup flour
- 1 tbsp vanilla extract
- 1 tsp instant espresso (optional)
- Pinch of kosher salt
- 9in (23cm) frozen pie shell
- Whipped cream, to serve

1. Preheat the oven to 375°F (190°C).
2. In a microwave-safe bowl, add the butter and chocolate. Microwave in 30-second intervals, stirring vigorously between each, until smooth and melted, about 2 or 3 times.
3. Let cool slightly, then whisk in the eggs, sugar, flour, vanilla, instant espresso (if using), and salt.
4. Place the pie shell on a rimmed baking sheet and pour in the filling. Bake for 45 to 50 minutes. A crust should form on the pie's surface (there will be some cracks, and that's okay!) but the filling should still jiggle very slightly at the center. Let cool for at least 1 hour before serving with the whipped cream.

don't mess it up!

This is such an easy recipe that it's almost impossible to mess up, but one way to do so is burning the chocolate. Since the heat on each microwave is different, a more fool-proof method is the double boiler—placing the butter and chocolate in a heat-proof bowl on top of a saucepan that contains a small amount of simmering water, which gently steams from below. However, because that requires me using an extra pan, I usually just stick with the microwave method and watch it carefully.

key lime tiramisu

Key lime pie reviews are kind of my thing: I've weighed in on pretty much every single version throughout the Florida Keys on my social media accounts. The truth is, those who can't do, critique. I've never successfully made a key lime pie at home. I live in the key lime pie capital of the world, so I really don't need to! But I have worked to perfect this variation on classic tiramisu, using traditional whipped mascarpone cream and ladyfingers paired with the beautiful tang of a key lime pie. It's a no-bake summer dessert miracle! Enjoy it with some Key Lime Painkillers (page 242), and you've got my dream date. Cute.

prep time
20 minutes, plus chilling time

yield
serves 8

- 2 cups heavy cream
- 1lb (450g) mascarpone cheese
- Zest and juice of 12 key limes, about ½ cup of key lime juice (or use 6 regular limes)
- 14oz (397g) can sweetened condensed milk
- 2 tsp vanilla extract
- 7oz (200g) package ladyfingers (24 cookies)
- ¾ cup key lime rum cream, such as Blue Chair Bay (see note)
- Graham cracker crumbs, to serve

1. In a large bowl, add the heavy cream and mascarpone. Using a hand mixer on low speed, whip for 30 seconds to combine, then turn the speed up to medium and whip for another 2 minutes, until soft peaks begin to form (see note below). Add the key lime zest (reserving some to garnish) and juice, condensed milk, and vanilla, and whip on medium speed for another 30 seconds to a minute just to combine.
2. In a 9 x 9-inch (23 x 23cm) baking dish, add about ⅓ of the key lime whipped cream. Add the key lime rum cream to a medium bowl or rimmed plate and, one at a time, dip each ladyfinger in the rum for 5 to 8 seconds to moisten, then layer 12 of them on top of the cream. Add another layer of the whipped cream, and repeat until you have 2 layers of ladyfingers and 3 layers of cream.
3. Cover with aluminum foil and chill in the refrigerator overnight, or for at least 6 hours. Serve with a sprinkle of graham cracker crumbs and the reserved key lime zest on top.

don't mess it up!

If you overwhip the mascarpone cream, it will develop a grainy texture that you can't come back from. "Soft peaks" means the cream will hold its shape but droop over when you turn the beater upside down. (I use the shape of the mountain from the original Grinch cartoon as my visual reference, in case that's helpful for you.) I don't like to take it further than that for this recipe, because the softer cream will absorb more easily into the ladyfingers.

ingredient intel

Can't find key lime rum cream? Make your own by combining ¼ cup each of cream, key lime juice, rum, and water, and 3 tablespoons of sugar.

30ish minutes

6 ingredients

one dish

pistachio amaretto affogato

prep time
10 minutes

yield
makes 4

4fl oz (120ml) amaretto
4 scoops pistachio gelato
4 biscotti or amaretti cookies
4fl oz (120ml) hot espresso or coffee
Chopped pistachios, to garnish

My number-one dinner-party rule is that if you don't know what to serve for dessert, serve affogato. In its purest form, it's a shot of hot espresso poured over a simple scoop of vanilla gelato or ice cream. It gives your guests a sugar rush and a caffeine boost all at the same time. I spike pistachio gelato with amaretto for a dessert-coffee-cocktail trifecta that will send your guests back out into the world feeling pretty damn good.

Divide the amaretto and gelato over 4 short glasses or small bowls. Place a biscotto in each glass, then pour over the hot espresso and garnish with the pistachios.

choose your own adventure

I love to experiment with different versions of this recipe using other flavors of gelato and various liquor options. Around the holidays, I'll do one with chocolate gelato and peppermint schnapps, which kind of tastes like a peppermint mocha coffee. Another one of my favorites is butter pecan ice cream or gelato with a splash of dark rum!

6 ingredients

no chop

one dish

basil limoncello spritz

Limoncello is a wonderfully sweet, slightly tart lemony liqueur I first fell in love with on a trip to Italy . . . pavilion, at Epcot. There's a little limoncello bar there, and I don't know why more Disney adults don't talk about it! This digestif is traditionally made by infusing a neutral spirit with lemon peels and sugar for a couple of weeks. Store-bought limoncellos are too sweet for me, so I like to go with a spritz. A touch more vodka, with sparkling wine and water, helps temper the sugar (and, I should warn you, makes the drink stronger). The fresh basil has citrusy notes that perfectly complement the lemon, but I've also made these with mint for a more fragrant finish.

prep time
10 minutes, plus chilling time

yield
makes 6 cocktails

12fl oz (350ml) limoncello
4fl oz (120ml) vodka
1 cup loosely packed fresh basil leaves, torn, plus whole sprigs to garnish
1 bottle prosecco
Club soda
Lemon wheels, to garnish

1. In a small pitcher, add the limoncello, vodka, and basil. Let chill in the fridge for at least 2 hours to infuse the basil.
2. When ready to serve, divide the infused limoncello evenly among 6 glasses filled with ice. Top with equal parts prosecco and club soda. Garnish with lemon wheels and basil sprigs.

30ish minutes

6 ingredients

no chop

one dish

frozen key lime painkillers

prep time
15 minutes

yield
makes 4 cocktails

4fl oz (120ml) dark rum
8fl oz (240ml) key lime rum cream, such as Blue Chair Bay
3 cups frozen pineapple
2fl oz (60ml) orange juice
1 tsp ground nutmeg, plus more to serve
Lime wedges, to serve
½ cup graham cracker crumbs, to serve

The first time I drank a painkiller was in the Bahamas on a family vacation. It's a harmonious blend of strong and fruity rum, bright citrus juices, creamy coconut, plus a hint of nutmeg for warmth in the finish. I can neither confirm nor deny whether I was of legal drinking age in the Bahamas at the time, but I was definitely not of age in the United States, and I was really going to town on those things. Needless to say, it took me a long time to revisit this frozen cocktail, but after moving to a tropical island and discovering all the incredible rum cocktails out there, I'm back, baby. This recipe spotlights my favorite key lime rum cream, giving it that local flair and one more interesting layer of citrus to go with the orange and pineapple.

1. In a blender, add the rum, rum cream, frozen pineapple, orange juice, nutmeg, and 2 cups ice. Blend until smooth.
2. Swirl a lime wedge around the rims of 4 glasses. Add the graham cracker crumbs to a plate and dip the rim of each glass into the crumbs. Pour in the drinks and garnish each with a lime wedge and a sprinkle of nutmeg.

use it up!

To finish that bottle of key lime rum cream, use it to soak the ladyfingers for my Key Lime Tiramisu (page 237).

30ish minutes
6 ingredients
no chop
one dish

frozen irish coffee milkshake

I first fell in love with frozen Irish coffee at a place called Molly's at the Market in the French Quarter of New Orleans, and that infatuation only grew stronger after I found a version here in Key West at Mary Ellen's bar, where they top the cocktail with crushed Oreos. This at-home replica has a smooth, milkshake-like consistency that requires only four ingredients, plus Oreos, which I say are optional . . . but if you want to really take the richness to the next level, don't skip them.

prep time
10 minutes

yield
makes 4 cocktails

- 16fl oz (475ml) cold-brew coffee
- 8fl oz (240ml) Bailey's Irish Cream
- 6fl oz (175ml) Irish whiskey, such as Jameson
- 1 pint vanilla ice cream
- Crushed Oreo cookies (optional)

In a blender, add the cold brew, Irish cream, whiskey, vanilla ice cream, and 3 cups ice. Blend until smooth, adding more ice if necessary to achieve your desired consistency. Divide over 4 glasses and top with the crushed Oreos, if using.

keep it chill

To keep frozen cocktails like this one or my Frozen Key Lime Painkillers (page 242) super frosty for as long as possible, freeze the serving glasses for at least 30 minutes ahead of time.

teeny-tiny pomegranate manhattinis

30ish minutes
6 ingredients
no chop
one dish

prep time
10 minutes

yield
makes 8 mini cocktails

8fl oz (240ml) bourbon
5 dashes bitters, preferably Peychaud's
2fl oz (60ml) pomegranate juice
Pomegranate seeds, to garnish
Rosemary sprigs, to garnish

At a certain point in my mid-twenties, I realized that taking shots was no longer dignified, so it was time for a rebrand: Teeny-Tiny Martinis. What had become déclassé was suddenly elegant. Restrained, even. And what's great is that anything can be a Teeny-Tiny Martini, if you put it in a teeny-tiny martini glass. These are about 2-fluid-ounce (60ml) pours, so even if you consume three, you'll be at about a standard martini consumption that you can feel classy about. Anything more than that . . . you're on your own, kid.

This is a pomegranate riff on a Manhattan that I love to serve around the holidays because the pomegranate seeds and rosemary resemble teeny-tiny sprigs of mistletoe.

In a cocktail shaker filled with ice, add the bourbon, bitters, and pomegranate juice and shake vigorously until chilled. Divide evenly among 4 mini martini glasses, pouring 2 to 3 fluid ounces (60 to 90ml) into each. Garnish with the pomegranate seeds and rosemary sprigs.

ingredient intel

Peychaud's bitters have a delightful warming anise flavor (they are traditionally used in the classic New Orleans cocktail, the Sazerac) that really complements the bourbon and keeps you coming back for another sip.

teeny-tiny texas tinis

30ish minutes
6 ingredients
no chop
one dish

prep time
10 minutes

yield
makes 8 mini cocktails

8fl oz (240ml) tequila
4fl oz (120ml) lime juice
2fl oz (60ml) fresh orange juice
1 tbsp agave
1 tbsp pickled jalapeño brine
Lime wedges, to garnish

Pretty much every Tex-Mex restaurant in my hometown of Austin serves some version of the "Texas Martini" or "Mexican Martini," which is generally made like a margarita but chilled in a cocktail glass with olive brine, which is not my thing (sorry to all you dirty martini lovers—more for you), so I use pickled jalapeño brine instead for a little spicy kick.

In a cocktail shaker filled with ice, add the tequila, lime juice, orange juice, agave, and jalapeño brine. Shake vigorously until chilled. Divide among 4 mini martini glasses and garnish each with a lime wedge.

don't mess it up!

Most bottled orange juices from the supermarket have sugar levels that will make these way too sweet, so it's important to use freshly squeezed orange juice straight from the fruit for this.

acknowledgments

This book is a dream come true that's been over a decade in the making, and I can't possibly thank everyone who helped make it finally come to life . . . but okay, I'll try.

First and foremost: My husband and momager, James. You've been my number one supporter since you showed up to my culinary school graduation twelve years ago when we were barely dating, and now we've created the most fun life I could ever imagine together. There's no one else on Earth I would be able to hang out with every single day without ending up on *Dateline*.

My agent, Tom Flannery, thank you for reaching out to me and being relentless in encouraging me to finish my book proposal even when I didn't want to and would ghost you for months. Your belief in me gave me the confidence to move forward and create a cookbook I am so proud of, and it wouldn't exist without your persistence.

Maura Cusick, my best friend, silly rabbit, and right-hand arm, you have a beautiful mind and are the reason this book looks absolutely gorgeous. Thanks for letting me steal you away from your job as an Emmy-nominated Hollywood costume designer to be our prop stylist. No one else could have had the creative vision and dedication to pull off that sparkly Teeny Tiny Martini tree.

My other best friend, my mom, who's always been on my side . . . even when I was wrong. Your only flaw is that you won't listen to Taylor Swift with me so you don't know those are her lyrics, but they still apply to us, and I want you to know you're my favorite person in the whole world. Thank you for always knowing the right thing to say to make me feel better and help me navigate life.

Dad, so much of your life's work has been advising people on how to make a living doing what they love to do, and I wouldn't have had the courage to follow this career path if I did not have the blessing of free, unlimited access to your wisdom my whole life. Your eternal optimism and kindness to everyone gets on my nerves sometimes, but that's only because I want to be more like you.

To my big sisters: Courtney, I still remember sitting in the kitchen with you saying I was scared to tell Mom and Dad I wanted to go to culinary school instead of law school. You encouraged me and said we would tell them that night after a bottle of wine. (This was merely a year after we executed the same attack strategy to tell them I was gay, so thank you for standing by me during my most vulnerable moments.) Ashley, I am in awe of your ability to travel the country doing a job that is so consequential, exhausting, and inspiring, all while raising Charlie and Scarlett to be the coolest nephew and niece I could've asked for, and still getting up at 5 a.m. every day for your miles-long runs. Our lifestyles couldn't possibly be more different, but I draw so much inspiration from your work ethic, and I'm sorry there aren't more ultra-healthy recipes for you in here.

Ree Drummond, thank you for being a professional inspiration to me for a decade before you even knew I existed. They say don't meet your heroes, but you proved that saying wrong. I'm so grateful for your friendship and willingness to write such a lovely foreword for this book without hesitation.

My amazing editor, Alexander Rigby, and everyone else on the team at DK, thank you for betting on me and giving me the creative leeway to make a cookbook that reflects my chaotic personality . . . while reining me in *just* enough.

Mackenzie Smith and Maite Aizpurua—the fiercest food photographer and food stylist duo! You took my vision for these photos and executed them better than I could have imagined in my wildest dreams, and we had so much fun doing it. Sunnie and Janai, we couldn't have done it without you! Romi Burianova, your lifestyle photography sprinkled the magic of Key West throughout the book and tied it all together in the most vibrant way.

Crosby Fitzgerald and Mary Mullally, thanks for showing up, showing out, and looking fabulous for our photo shoot.

All my friends who volunteered their time to test or taste these recipes for this book to make sure they were perfect . . . Morgan, Carlee, Carly, Cassie, Maddy, Justin, Malcolm, Emily (and all of the Milwaukee Hirsch family), Chris, Megan, Meaghan, Maria, Ana, Noelle, Tautin, Sarah, Trixie, Rachael, Amber, Other Amber, Janelle (and all the Currins and Hornblowers), Evan, Sam, Isabelle, Wyatt, Danielle, Jessica, Shoshie, Carole, Amy, Julie, Isabella, Jule, Haley, Audrey, Kitty, Mud, Mud Jr, Jane, Klem, Schulz . . . and your lovely family members who helped in the kitchen! I love you and thank you all.

To those who helped me in my career when I had no experience, namely Janet McCracken and Nina Elder, who gave me my first big break by hiring me at the Rachael Ray test kitchen—so many of my fondest professional memories involve you two. Sonal Dutt, thank you for giving me my dream job at *People* magazine, and allowing me to have amazing opportunities to chase the stories I wanted to and work with fabulous colleagues and friends like Ana Calderone, Colleen Kratofil, and Maria Yagoda.

Everyone who has followed, liked, shared, or left a nice comment on my social media channels over the years, thank you for supporting me. This book would not have been possible without you, and I get emotional thinking about how so many people whom I've never met in real life have changed my life immeasurably.

To my Godparents, Cissy and Tim, who have shown me so much love and support over the years. And my Grandparents—Martha, Joe, Ruth, and Big Roy—all of whom I wish I'd had more time with in this life but are present throughout this book.

My late aunt Susan, who is the funniest person I've ever known and always hyped me up. I try to carry your energy with me every day, but there's no one in the world like you.

Finally, thank you to my only child, Eddie Martini. You make every day more joyful, even when you spend fifteen minutes each night barking at your own reflection in the door.

index

a–b

e

f

g

h

i–j

r

s

t

v

w–z

about the author

Shay Spence is a Texas-born food and travel writer with over a decade of experience in the culinary field. After attending the Institute of Culinary Education in New York City in 2014, Shay worked in the test kitchen for Rachael Ray's magazine, and then spent six years as the Food Editor for *People* magazine. He now works as a full-time social media food content creator, while continuing to write for *People*, *Food & Wine*, *Wine Enthusiast*, and various other publications. Over the past few years, Shay has amassed over 1.7 million followers on TikTok and 500,000 followers on Instagram by showcasing his creative recipes, favorite restaurants, and unique travel destinations through an expert lens. Shay was a contestant on the second season of Gordon Ramsay's *Next Level Chef* on Fox, and he currently lives in Key West, Florida, with his husband, James, and their pup, Eddie Martini.